Contents

Spelling & language skills

ANGELA REDFERN

Published by Scholastic Publications Ltd,
Villiers House,
Clarendon Avenue,
Leamington Spa,
Warwickshire CV32 5PR

© 1993 Scholastic Publications Ltd
Reprinted 1994

Author Angela Redfern
Editor Juliet Gladston
Series designer Joy White
Designer Micky Pledge
Illustrations Liz Thomas
Cover illustration Frances Lloyd
Cover photograph Martyn Chillmaid

Designed using Aldus Pagemaker
Processed by Pages Bureau, Leamington Spa
Artwork by David Harban Design, Warwick
Printed in England by Clays Ltd, St Ives plc

British Library Cataloguing-in-Publication Data
A catalogue record for this book is
available from the British Library.

ISBN 0-590-53078-X

Why explore language?

The Kingman Report of March 1988 provided a forceful reminder that language is a subject of interest and, indeed, a subject for study in its own right. Kingman stressed that, from their earliest years, children are fascinated by language – by rhythms, rhymes and repetitive patterns. This is an interest which, if encouraged, will expand to embrace puns, double meanings, tongue-twisters, anagrams, palindromes – indeed word games of every possible kind.

The Kingman model also included discussion of the differences between spoken and written language, idioms, metaphors, historical and geographical language variations and what English owes to other languages via derivations and borrowings. This knowledge about language was seen as every child's entitlement, a source of enrichment and empowerment.

The Cox Report of November 1988 took up the points from the Kingman Report and offered further recommendations about language variety, the relationship between the reader and the writer, and about how best to make a message clear.

How to set about doing it?

Language

Both the Kingman and Cox Reports were quick to point out that old-style isolated grammar exercises were not the best way to teach language skills. Instead they strongly supported teaching through the exploration of pupils' language in use.

The role of the teacher, therefore, becomes one of constructive intervention, enabling children to become aware of their own and others' use of language.

Spelling

Children pass through a number of stages on their way to becoming efficient spellers.
• Stage one: random letters are used to express meaning.
• Stage two: letter-sound correspondence is attempted, for example 'cts' for 'carrots'.
• Stage three: all sounds are represented phonetically, for example 'sez' for 'says'.
• Stage four: children move from a dependence on sounds to a reliance on visual patterns, using analogies with known words, for example 'clime' for 'climb'.
• Stage five: correct conventional forms are used with words being visualised in the mind.

Thus, it is important to remember that inventive spellings are a natural step along the spelling route and that errors may well signal progress. However, children should be encouraged to become active learners as regards spelling just as in other areas of learning. They should:
• 'look with intent' and take mental photos of words in order to develop visual memory;
• write words down to see if they look right;
• use the 'look–cover–write–check' technique;
• link handwriting and spelling to get common letter patterns into the hand;
• hunt for word groups and common clusters;
• make collections of words of specific interest.

Savouring language in this ongoing way can give children a genuine thirst for exploring language that will stay with them throughout their lives.

What exactly to teach?

The various English National Curriculum documents have specified the requirements in relation to spelling and language skills.

Key Stage 1 – Children should:
• play with language, making up jingles, riddles, word games; play I-Spy and experiment with alliteration;
• learn the names and order of the letters of the alphabet, upper and lower case, and how to write their own names;
• pay close attention to spelling patterns and word families and learn to spell common simple words;
• experiment with spelling and discuss misapplied generalisations and other reasons for misspellings;
• use wordbooks and dictionaries;
• learn terminology such as capital, full stop, vowel, consonant, verb, noun;
• begin to check their own writing for accuracy.

Key Stage 2 – Children should:
• experiment with sound effects, verbal rhymes and rhythms;
• be adventurous with vocabulary;
• accumulate a growing bank of words they can spell correctly;
• use their knowledge of letter patterns to check spellings and meanings of words in a dictionary and realise the relevance of roots of words, for example loveliness under lovely;
• learn the use, meaning and spelling of common prefixes and suffixes, for example -able, -ness, -ful;
• learn to recognise silent letters and alternative ways of spelling the same sound, for example gn, kn, pn, mn;
• learn about inflectional endings, for example trapped, coming, beaded;
• learn to use an apostrophe to spell shortened

forms, for example, don't, they've;
- memorise visual patterns of irregular spellings;
- understand when it is appropriate to use standard English and dialect.

Progression
- Level 1 – Children begin to pay attention to visual patterns and to remember the spelling of familiar words
- Level 2 – Children recognise the basic conventions of the English spelling system, and spell simple monosyllabic words correctly.
- Level 3 – Children use capitals consistently, spell correctly words with common prefixes and suffixes, and regular polysyllabic words, and begin to proof-read their own work.
- Level 4 – Children spell correctly complex polysyllabic words with regular patterns, for example medical; use apostrophes to indicate shortened forms, and break longer words into more manageable units to assist spelling.
- Level 5 – Children remember the visual patterns of irregular spellings, spell correctly words with inflectional suffixes that require doubling or vowel deletion.

It is important to realise that these levels are by no means watertight. They depend very much on the previous linguistic experiences of the children and the interest of teachers.

Of course, we must also bear in mind the distinction between implicit and explicit knowledge about language. The class teacher is the person with the greatest knowledge about individual children's language expertise and it is her responsibility to decide when to encourage children to reflect on their language use and to begin the process of moving from implicit knowledge to full reflective awareness, which is the ultimate goal for fluent writers.

Implications for the classroom

There are three main areas regarding the activities in this book that need to be highlighted, namely: the role of talk; the grouping of children; and the outcomes of the work.

Role of talk
The National Oracy Project has demonstrated that, for AT1 to be a reality, it is essential to create a climate in the classroom where talk is valued as an integral part of planning, responding, reflecting and sharing work, and where co-operation is actively encouraged. Many activities in this book can be undertaken as discussions by quite young children, although they may not be able to attempt them in writing without support. Older children or adults can act as scribes so that no one misses out because of inadequate secretarial skills.

For those children whose home language is not English, older children who speak the same language can be an invaluable support in discussion especially, though by no means exclusively, in the early days before full command of English is mastered. Discussion is every bit as valuable a part of the proceedings as the recording on paper afterwards. Activities focusing on language diversity also offer invaluable opportunities for emergent bilingual children to take on the role of the expert.

Working in groups
The National Oracy Project has provided a fund of information about the variety of possible strategies for grouping children.
- They can work individually. This may be because of a child's preference or because of a decision by the teacher.
- The children can work in pairs. This may be organised so that two children with similar approaches work together; two children who are at the same level of linguistic experience work together; two children at different levels of linguistic development work together, as a support for the one and an opportunity to lead for the other; two children with a common home language work together; two children of the same gender work together to offer security; two children of opposite gender work together; an adult and a child (opening up lots of possibilities for parents and the local community to play a part) work together.
- The children can work in small groups. There are similar reasons for deciding on the composition of the groups as for pair work.
- The children can work as a whole class in oral discussion. This can be done when the teacher feels the need to play a major role in the discussion, perhaps when launching an activity; when the teacher wishes to model a pattern of working for children to follow in future when working without the support of an adult; workshares when a whole class comes together to reflect on their experiences.

The decision as to how to organise the children when working on activities in this book, however, must remain with the teacher as it is he who knows how the children will work best.

Outcomes
The process approach to the teaching of writing as endorsed by the National Curriculum encourages children to plan, redraft if necessary, edit and publish chosen pieces of work, giving due consideration to choice of typeface, illustration, lay-out on the page, format for the required purpose and audience, cover design and so on. It is essential to encourage children to take an avid interest in exactly how their work should be displayed or published, whether it

could become a performance for the class or for a larger audience in a school assembly, whether it could transfer to another medium, for example on to a tape for the listening corner, or on to a video, if you are lucky enough to have access to a camcorder. Making decisions (and reflecting on their validity afterwards) is a crucial part of the learning process and making such decisions as these should be an integral part of every school's language provision.

Summing up

In no way are the activities in this book intended to be used as substitutes for the 'teacher as reader/child as writer' dialogues that arise regularly in the classroom. Rather, the activities provide an addition to and are not instead of such vital daily discussions. They can be used to form focused sessions where children's curiosity about language is excited. They can run in parallel with the ongoing practice of the classroom that provides so many opportunities for savouring language together – in story time, when hearing children read, when sharing work, when entertaining visiting writers and countless other fruitful moments for commenting on language in use (words, phrases, making comparisons, collecting sayings and so on).

Alphabet

The activities in this section cover the letters of the alphabet. As well as teaching letter recognition, sound-symbol relationships and alphabetical order, their aim is to enrich children's vocabulary and encourage them to collect as many words for each letter of the alphabet as possible. Young children often have a most extensive oral vocabulary, so don't limit them to only a few of the most obvious words.

Sometimes giving clues, miming words, reminding children of vocabulary from books will bring out a horde of half-remembered words.

Variations

It goes without saying that it is up to the class teacher to ring the changes with the activities suggested. The activity provided for the letter A (see page 11) would equally be valid for B, C, D and so on, just as the activity centred on B (see page 12) could be used for D, E and F. Indeed, all the activities suggested are interchangeable.

In line with National Curriculum requirements, upper and lower case letters are introduced together. Encourage children to think of vocabulary that requires capital letters as well as lower case ones, for example names of people, streets, towns, countries – especially those connected with their families (where they live, where they came from, where they moved to). The more personal the associations the greater the impact on the children and the more likely it will be that learning will take place. Each child's own name has, of course, great significance, so a special feature can be made of these as you progress through the alphabet.

Letter names

The National Curriculum, in step with recent research findings, recommends that both letter name and letter sound are introduced to children. Therefore, for the purpose of these activities vocabulary should not be restricted to sound associations only. We need to encourage children to get into the habit of looking at words carefully from the start (to encourage their visual memory). Thus apple, arm, aeroplane and angel would all be acceptable for the letter A.

Decoration

Decorating the page borders with letters is specifically mentioned only for the letter B (see page 12). It is important, however, to foster this habit throughout the book. The fast, free-flowing practice of letters and common letter strings to get them into the hand is highly beneficial.

Decorative borders also play a part in fostering children's pride in their work and in sowing the seeds for aesthetic discrimination such as choice of colours and general visual appeal on the page.

Writing for a purpose

The activity for the letter N (see page 24) introduces for the first time a published outcome and it is here that we begin the process of matching format to purpose and audience – in this case a poster. Later activities culminate in books of various kinds and the elements of DTP come into their own. Whenever there is a chance for display or publication – a collection of poems, stories or recipes – children should be encouraged to make choices and decisions about the suitability of format to purpose, of tone of voice to audience, about accessibility for the reader and visual appeal, for example typeface, headings, illustrations and layout on the page.

A global perspective

Language diversity must be an integral part of the classroom practice in all schools. Finding names from many cultures (see page 11) opens the door to a wider world perspective that should run through all the alphabet sessions. Restaurants, recipes, works of art, crafts, music, television, films, books, folk tales, holidays, visits and visitors all provide a wealth of opportunities to introduce a global perspective. Think carefully about the tone and choice of resources so as to avoid a patronising or stereotypical view. If you teach in a multicultural school, use the specialised knowledge of the children's families and your local community.

Organisation

In some classes, there will be children in the very early stages of making letter–sound relationships or holding visual images. Some teachers dip into the alphabet regularly in weekly whole-class oral sessions, feeling that some gains will be made from interaction with more experienced language users; some teachers offer visual props such as artefacts, actions, pictures to support understanding; other teachers work with small groups only when they feel that the work will be within the grasp of the children concerned. Whatever your own preferred way, do remember to praise near misses and encourage a fun approach to this aspect of exploring language as with all others.

Recording

Children can enjoy these alphabet activities in oral situations long before they can cope with recording them on their own. Decide whether to limit the sessions purely to discussion or whether to keep a written record with the help of an older child or an adult acting as scribe. There is no necessity for every single piece of work to be recorded, as children also need to understand that talking and thinking constitute valid activities in their own right. Many young children do appreciate a finished product, however, either hand-written or word processed by a scribe. The writing can be done at a later time to serve as a useful way to recap on the learning that has taken place. Don't expect total recall! Every little helps and can be built on in the future.

When they have completed their first written run through, children can keep all the initial letter sheets to make their own personal dictionary.

Other skills

Usually, children benefit from further wanders through the alphabet. There is no harm in a more advanced and confident child leading a small group of peers in a short oral session – the skills of communication and of group management are very useful ones to develop.

Encourage the habit of looking with intent by staging classroom hunts for letters and letter patterns. Take this golden opportunity to link the two worlds of home and school by extending searches out from the classroom into the home and community and to local libraries. As children progress, introduce the use of a dictionary, a thesaurus, and general reference books.

Alphabet answers

Page 21: king; kitten; kangaroo; kitchen; kettle; keep. Knife; knight; knock-knock; knuckle; knitting; knot.

Page 23: monster; mouse; mud/muck; monkey; moon; marigold; morning; magnet; mango; music.

Page 27: queen; quietly; quilt; quickly; quaint; quins; quiet; queue; question; quivering; quaking.

Page 34: fix; fox/fax; mix; cox; ox; wax; tax; pixie; box; flax; taxi; axe/oxo; exit; toxic;

Page 35: yak; you; yell; yeast; yearn; yummy; Yvonne; Yasmin; yourself; yoghurt; yolk; yippee; yours/years; yesterday; yellow; yonder; your; year; young; yodel.

Common letter patterns

This section moves on from the basic 26 letters of the alphabet to cover common letter patterns, such as consonant digraphs, blends, vowel digraphs and letter strings.

When working on the activities in this section it is important to encourage the children to continue making decorative page borders so that common letter strings become automatic. Also encourage them to order alphabetically whenever they collect words or organise picture dictionaries.

In this section the children must still hunt for letter patterns but this time with more stress on taking a mental photo and holding a mental image, which will help them to move from phonetic to visual reliance.

The activities also draw on children's strongly developing sense of fun, providing them with opportunities for playing with language, for example limericks, songs and mock interviews.

Recent research has shown syllabification to be of significance in learning to read. Work on syllabification is begun here (see page 50) and can, of course, be used with other letter patterns.

A further activity involving language variety is included (see page 51), preparing the ground for investigations in a later section of the patterns of usage of different languages and dialects.

Common letter patterns answers

Page 39: thank you; thumb; thunder; thief; thorns; three; thirteen; thermometer; thread; theatre; throne; thatch.

Page 41: c, d, f, g, p, t.

Page 42: c, f, g, p, s.

Page 49: guide; guilt; biscuit; suite; pursuit; bruises; cruise; buildings; suit; fruit juice.

Page 54: 1 = Peterborough/Slough etc; 2 = bough; 3 = tougher; 4 = coughing; 5 = ought; 6 = ploughed, rough; 7 = enough.

Page 56: crystal; abyss; myth; syllabus; symbol; pyramid; sympathy; oxygen; syrup; physics; sycamore; hypnotist; mystery; hymn; system; typical; cygnet; symmetry.

How the English language works

This section covers many common grammatical features under the general groupings of nouns, adjectives and verbs:

- nouns: abbreviations, compound nouns, common endings for nouns (see pages 65 to 72);
- adjectives: prefixes (see page 73); suffixes (see pages 74 to 79);
- verbs: endings (see pages 80 and 81); patterns (see page 82); doubling (see page 84); links between spelling and meaning (see page 86).

The habits established in the earlier sections should be developed further – decorative borders with a greater variety of letter patterns, alphabetical order becoming more automatic, taking mental photos and building an ever increasing store of known spellings. Children will probably be becoming more and more hooked on exploring language. Even so, when collecting words they will, at times, find ones whose meaning they are unsure of. As adults we too occasionally come across words that we only half grasp, but we may like the feel of the word on our tongue or its rhythmical beat, and half meanings can always develop into full understanding at a later date.

The aim of this section is to help children to make analogies by reflecting on the differences in written forms of language, for example, driver/baker/flyer (see page 65), happiness (see page 66), and by encouraging them to put language to use in a continuous piece, crafted to the best of their ability, for example creative writing, definitions for a dictionary, descriptions, newspaper articles and jokes.

Use of a dictionary is an increasing feature in this section. By doing so, children will gain valuable experience of dictionary conventions.

Linguistic terminology is also consolidated, for example prefix, suffix and verbs.

How the English language works answers
Page 59: BC = Before Christ; AD = After Christ;
a.m. = before noon; p.m. = after noon; AWOL = absent without leave; BBC = British Broadcasting Corporation; COD = cash on delivery; EC = European Community; HRH = Her/His Royal Highness; HM = Her/His Majesty or ; IOU = I owe you; ITV = Independent Television; NB = take note; PS = postscript; PTO = please turn over; RIP = rest in peace; RSVP = please answer; s.a.e. = stamped addressed envelope; UK = United Kingdom; UN = United Nations; USA = United States of America; VIP = very important person.

Page 60: asses; buffaloes; foxes; monkeys; mosquitoes; wives; ponies; wolves; oxen; mice; geese; cherries; matches; boxes; knives; spoons; loaves; potatoes; tomatoes; shoes; brushes; dominoes; shelves.

Page 62: 1 = yo-yo; 2 = see-saw; 3 = flip-flop.

Page 63: heliport; chunnel; Oxbridge; motel; brunch; cheeseburger; smog; ginormous; mizzle; orangeade.

Page 64: a bucketful of water; an armful of parcels; a mouthful of food; a fistful of money; a cupful of flour; a bagful of shopping; a plateful of chips; a pocketful of marbles.

Page 73: inaccurate; incapable; inconsiderate; incredible; independent; indirect; illegal; illogical; impolite; impossible; improbable; irregular. Immobile; inattentive; incorrect; inadequate; infinite; imperfect; inexpensive; irresponsible; inconvenient; incomplete.

Page 78: alphabetical; hysterical/comical; medical; theatrical; optical; vertical; tropical; political; magical; identical.

Language variety

More than any other section this is perhaps the one that can fire children's imagination. It is devoted entirely to language variety, which has permeated previous sections but now becomes the main focus. Whatever the composition of the school, work of this nature needs to be set within an ethos of anti-racist education. Classrooms should offer a wide range of materials, artefacts and literature that reflect the multicultural and multilingual nature of modern Britain. Dual text books, newspapers in various scripts, Chinese writing brushes and calligraphic pens should be part and parcel of every classroom.

This section includes activities which use ancient and modern scripts. These provide an ideal opportunity for those children whose home language is not written in Roman script to see their culture legitimised in the classroom and their skills valued (see pages 87 to 90).

Activities on dialects and languages other than English provide bilingual children with a chance to show their expertise (see pages 92 to 97). Attitudes towards dialects and bilingualism need to be seen as positive. Reflecting on their own language use enables children to grasp the complexity of the skills involved and it is a tremendous boost to their confidence when they see their own competence in this light.

The activites on derivations start from the basis that language is forever changing and that we all make a contribution to the changes that are being made. Children are intrigued by the fact that English has not always been as it is now, and take a delight in being linguistic detectives, spotting meaning with the help of derivations from other languages (see pages 98 to 107). There are many possibilities for work across the curriculum with codes, maps, surveys, myths and legends, historical and geographical aspects of settlers and invaders, personal lifelines and migration patterns. Reasons for moving, feelings about moving, coping with new social and cultural settings, missing old friends, making new ones, the loss of confidence when faced with a different language or dialect – all offer opportunities for discussion and writing.

The rest of the activities look at borrowings, reflecting on the rich mixture of English. Words are seen to cross frontiers as populations merge and mix (see pages 108 to 113). Draw on children's personal experiences with the family, on holiday, from television, penpals and so on.

Language variety answers

Page 88: Can you meet me in London tomorrow?

Page 91: taka/paise; yuan/fen; franc/centimes; mark/pfennigs; drachma/lepta; rupee/paise; shekel/agorot; lira/centesimi; yen/sen; shilling/cents; krona/öre; escudo/centavos; rouble/kopeks; peseta/centimos; dollar/cents.

Page 93: Dutch = water; French = eau; Greek = νερο; Hindi = pani; Spanish = agua; English = water; Russian = вода; German = wasser; Italian = acqua; Latin = aqua; Portuguese = aqua.

Page 99: Celts = bog, clan, coracle, glen, loch, macintosh, tweed, whisky; Romans = album, circus, consul, exit, forum, genius, January, miser, rostrum, street; Vikings = bairn, crooked, fellow, hit, husband, knife, saga, skin, take, want, wrong; Greeks = axis, chorus, crisis, cycle, delta, gymnasium, idea, idiot, myth, orchestra.

Page 101: triangle; tricycle; tripod; tricolour; trident; trio; trillion; triplets.

Page 102: percent; centurion; centimes; century; centimetre; centenary; bicentennial; centigrade; centipede; centilitre.

Page 104: antecedent; antechamber; antediluvian; posterity; postgraduate; posthumous; antemeridiem/postmeridiem; postnatal/antenatal; postpone; postscript; postwar.

Page 105: multi-storey; semi-detached; multitude; semicircle; multimillionaire; semi-conscious; multilingual; semi-final; multicoloured; semiquaver/semibreve; multi-purpose; semi-permanent; multicultural; semi-darkness; multiply; semiprecious.

Page 108: samosa = Indian; blinis = Russian; moussaka = Greek; pizza = Italian

Page 111: polo; chutney; khaki; dungarees; shampoo; jodhpurs; pyjamas; jungle; bungalow; gymkhana; curry; bangle; catamaran; yoga; dinghy.

Page 112: Native American = canoe, moccasin, potato, tomato, totem; Cowboys = bonanza, colt, corral, mustang, stetson; Modern USA = drive-in, hamburger, hot dog, penthouse, skyscraper.

Page 113: algebra = Greek; boss = American; chalet = Swiss French; devil = Greek; éclair = French; forum = Latin; geyser = Icelandic; hobble = Middle English; interval = Latin; ju-jitsu = Japanese; kiosk = Turkish/Persian; leprachaun = Irish; museum = Greek; nadir = Arabic; outlaw = Old English; panda = Nepalese; quadruped = Latin; rumour = Latin; sauna = Finnish; tom-tom = Hindi; ugly = Viking; voodoo = Dahomey; walkabout = Australian; Xavier = Spanish; yoga = Indian; zero = French.

Playing with language

This section is given over to the joys of word-play, although it also reinforces many aspects which have been previously introduced. Follow-up activities offer a range of outcomes such as writing stories, making books for younger children (particularly enabling for bilingual children and those less confident than others of their age), quizzes, illustrations, rhyming couplets and so on.

Some of the games are based on alphabetical order but can be developed in more sophisticated ways as children's expertise increases. For example, children can debate their final publication choices, apply more complex rules and introduce time limits for games to engender a feeling of extra excitement. Young children can also have fun playing these games. They should work in a group situation with an adult to support them with their final publication.

Other word games are based on playing with individual letters or patterns, for example the, act. This same activity is valid for any letter pattern that occurs within words.

This section also includes games based on rhyme. Rhyme is very important in the early stages of learning to read, thus these games should be played communally either in small groups or as whole class sessions. A co-operative publication could result.

The rest of the games in this section are associated with the sounds of the language – onomatopoeia, spoonerisms, homophones, alliteration, puns – or with meaning – synonyms, antonyms, homographs, similes, figures of speech, sayings. With adult support, many of these activities are suitable for young children.

Playing with language answers

Page 122: lake; pond; flood; sea; puddle; stream; rain; river; canoe; shower; pool.

Page 126: radar; level; civic.

Page 129: mouth; feet; wife; head; look; eyes; road; knees; table.

Page 135: I leaned over; you go first; kneel down; gymnastics; loose elastic; horse and cart; call in anytime; antiques; bet he doesn't.

Page 136: please; crane; train.

Page 140: row; bow; sow; lead; reading.

Name _____

❖ Think of **all** the people you know whose name begins with **A** and write them below. It could be their first name or their family name. Don't forget to start each name with **a** capital letter!

Girls	Boys
Mrs Armitage Ann	Ahmed Allan Ahlberg

Don't forget the people:
• in your family;
• in your class;
• in your street;
• on the television;
• in books;
• who write books.
Don't forget your pets!

❖ Find out why your name was chosen for you.

❖ Find out if it has **a** special meaning.

Name _____

Bb

✤ **B**e a **b**usy **b**ee and **b**rainstorm with a partner all the verbs – that's things you can do – **b**eginning with **b**. Write them **b**elow.

Bb

bake _____

_____

_____

_____

_____

_____

_____

boil _____

_____

_____

_____

_____

_____

_____

build _____

_____

_____

_____

_____

_____

_____

✤ Mime one of your verbs and see if your friends can guess it correctly. Take it in turns and go through your lists.

✤ **B**orders can **be b**eautiful. Make a **b**order of **bbb**s round the edge of this sheet.

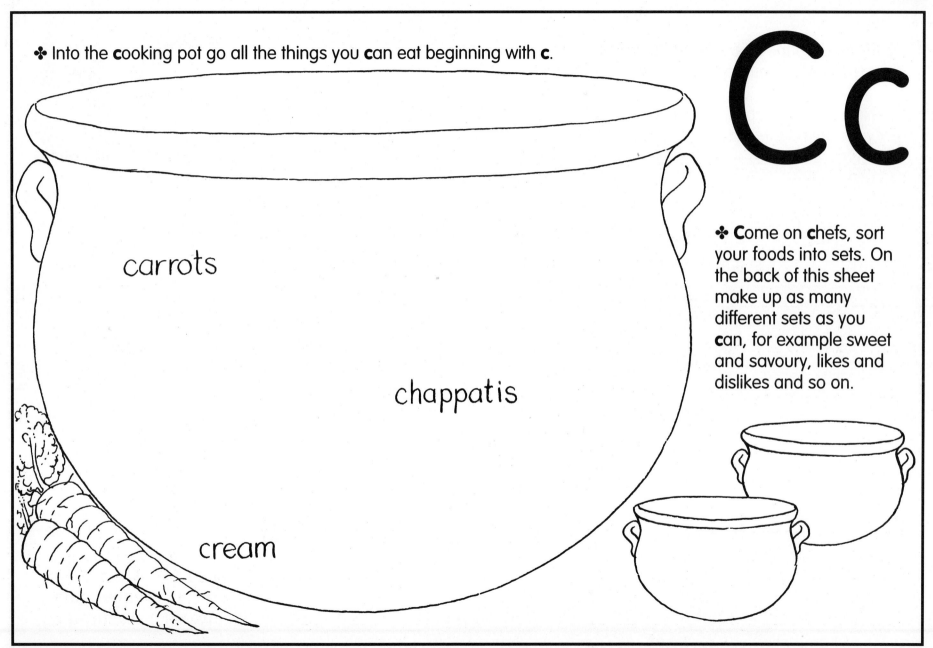

✤ Into the **c**ooking pot go all the things you **c**an eat beginning with **c**.

carrots

chappatis

cream

✤ **C**ome on **c**hefs, sort your foods into sets. On the back of this sheet make up as many different sets as you **c**an, for example sweet and savoury, likes and dislikes and so on.

Name _____

Dd

The hunt is on for **adjectives**. These are words that **describe**, that tell us what someone or something is like.

♣ Fill the treasure chest with adjectives that begin with **d**. A **d**ictionary might help!

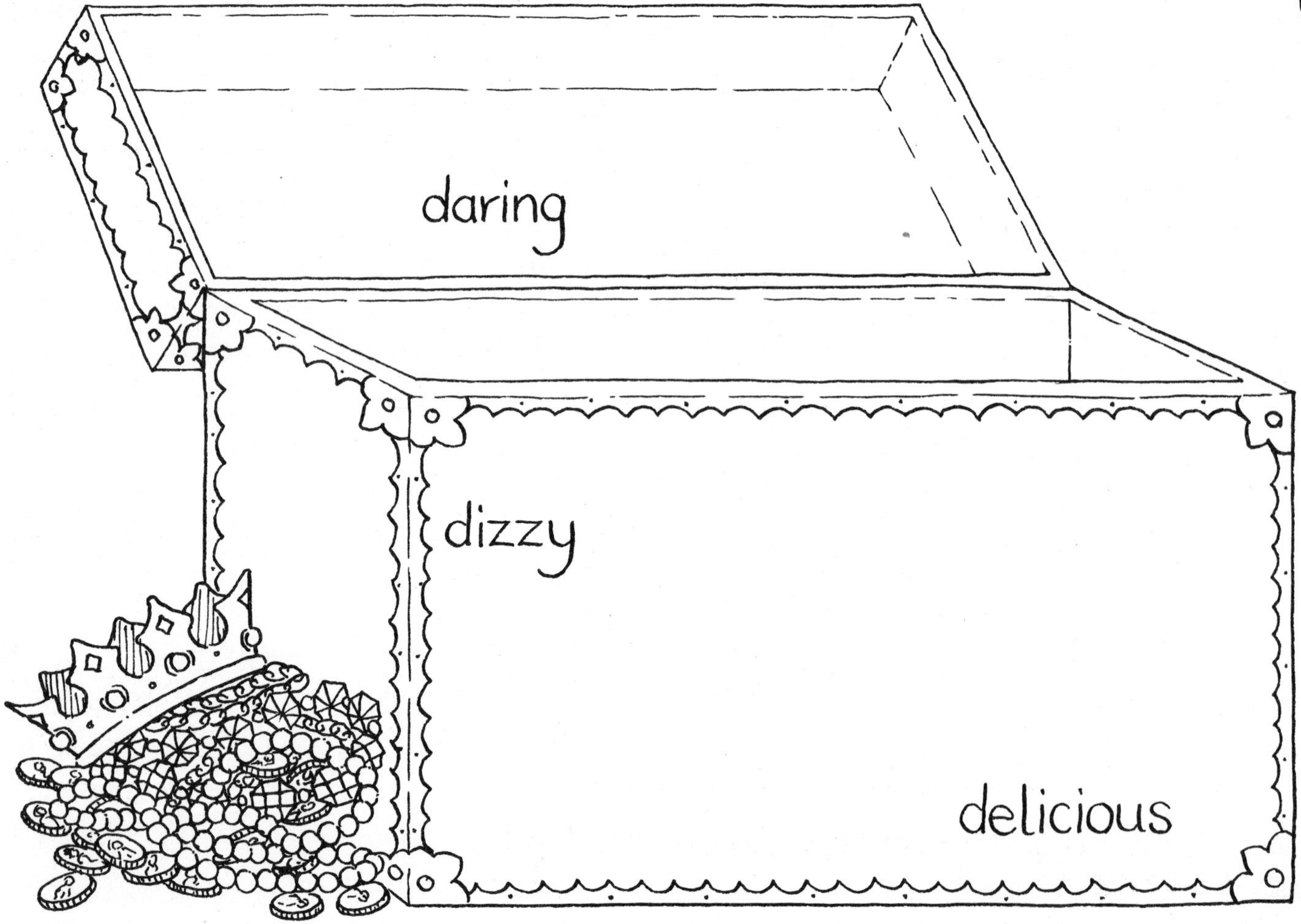

daring

dizzy

delicious

♣ Choose your favourite adjective and illustrate it here.

♣ Turn this sheet over and **d**o a few more.

Teacher Timesavers: Spelling and language skills

♣ Write down as many places as you can find which begin with capital **E**.

Ee

Countries
Ethiopia

Towns
Edinburgh

Streets/Roads
Eastern Avenue

Knowing where to look for **e**xtra ideas is very important. Have you tried an atlas? A street map? A telephone directory?

Name _____

Ff

✤ **F**ill the boxes below as **f**ast as you can with words that begin with **f**.
Ready, steady, go!

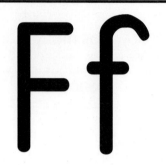

Nouns	Verbs
finger 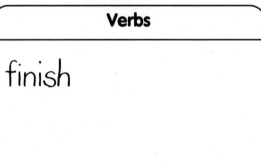	finish
Fred	

Adjectives

full

✤ Turn this page over and have another go.

❖ Have you noticed that in very old books letters were often beautifully decorated?

❖ Make the large **G** below as attractive as you can, like a **g**lorious old manuscript.

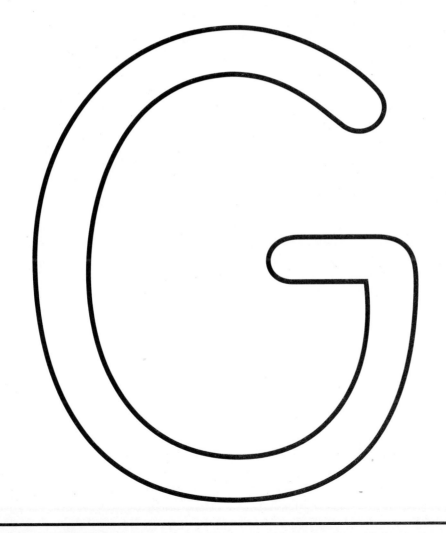

❖ Make a collection of book titles which have **g** words in them. Here are some to **g**et you **g**oing:
• **G**oldilocks and the three Bears,
• Mr **G**umpy's Outing,
• **G**randpa.

❖ Write a review of one of these books that will make your friends rush off to read it.

Hh

♣ **H**ave a go with a friend at making up some **h**ilarious stories, where the main words begin with **h**. Look at the example below then cut out the two blank panels.

♣ Write the first word, fold back the paper and swap with your friend. **H**ave fun reading your stories to each other, when you've finished.

Ask yourself:

• **who?**

• **did what?**

• **where?**

• **when?**

• **why?**

Harpal		
hurried		
to the hut		
at half past four		
to have a hard-boiled egg		

Name _____

✤ Look at the word triangle below. Can you spot the pattern?

✤ Now make your own pattern using different words.
Each word has to begin with **i**.

1 | I
2 | i s
3 | i n k
4 | i n t o
5 | i g l o o
6 | i n s i d e
7 | i n t e n s e
8 | i n t e r e s t
9 | i n v i s i b l e
10 | i m p o s s i b l e

1 | I _____
2 | _____
3 | _____
4 | _____
5 | _____
6 | _____
7 | _____
8 | _____
9 | _____
10 | _____

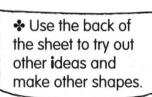

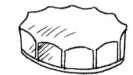

✤ Use the back of the sheet to try out other **i**deas and make other shapes.

Name _____

Jj

✤ Turn over this sheet and brainstorm some j words.

✤ Join a friend and write a story about Jason, Jaswinder or Jean.
Every sentence **must** contain one word beginning with j.

One day last June, _____

_____

_____

_____

_____

_____

_____

_____

_____

Jj

Not many words in English begin with **k**.

♣ Use the clues to help you find some of them.

• I married the queen.

___ ___ ___ ___

• I'm a baby cat.

___ ___ ___ ___ ___ ___

• I'm a good jumper.

___ ___ ___ ___ ___ ___ ___

• I'm full of pots and pans.

___ ___ ___ ___ ___ ___ ___

• Polly put me on.

___ ___ ___ ___ ___ ___ ___

• I'm part of a Norman castle.

___ ___ ___ ___ ___

♣ Solve the clues to discover some tricky **k** words. Why are they tricky?

• I cut bread.

___ ___ ___ ___ ___

• I wear shining armour.

___ ___ ___ ___ ___ ___

• Who's there?

___ ___ ___ ___ ___ ___ ___ ___

• I'm part of your hand.

___ ___ ___ ___ ___ ___ ___

• You need two needles for me.

___ ___ ___ ___ ___ ___

• Tie me!

___ ___ ___ ___

Kk

Quite a lot of names begin with **K**.

♣ List as many as you can.

Kate
Kamaljit
Klaus

Name _____

Ll

LL

♣ Play this game with some friends. Each word must start with the letter L – see how many you can think of:

Boy's name

Girl's name

Town

Country

River

Mountain

Animal

Bird

Fruit

Vegetable

Tree

Flower

♣ Continue the story below. Don't forget to use lots of l words.

Lester had a twin sister called Lesley. They lived in a lovely flat in a little town near a lake... _____

_____

_____

_____

_____

_____

_____

♣ Try it with other letters.

_____

Name _____

❧ Solve the clues to discover the words beginning with **m**.

You have one **m**inute, starting NOW...

A scary creature: _____

A tiny squeaking
creature: _____

Pigs roll in it: _____

A jungle animal: _____

It goes round the earth: _____

A flower: _____

Early in the day: _____

It attracts iron: _____

A tropical fruit: _____

We dance to it: _____

❧ **M**ake up your own set of
m clues and try them out on
your friends.

Mm

_____

_____

_____

_____

_____

_____

_____

_____

❧ Did you notice these answers are all nouns? You can **m**ake clues for verbs too.

Name _____

Nn

♣ Design a poster setting out rules for being a good **n**eighbour.
Draft your ideas below.

○

Never

Never

Never

Never

Never

Never

Never

Nn

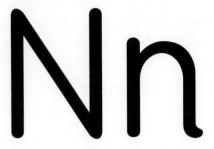

♣ To make your poster eye-catching, you **n**eed to think carefully about:
• the choice of colours;
• tone (serious or amusing);
• size and style of lettering;
• illustrations.

♣ **O**K it's **o**ver to you: write down all the **o** words you can think of. **O**rganise them into lists below.

People	Places	Nouns	Verbs	Adjectives	Extras
Omar	Oldham	owl	offer	odd	out

♣ Now turn **o**ver this sheet and play Hangman with a friend using words from your lists.

Name _____

Pp

Tongue-twisters are hard to say but **p**ractice makes **p**erfect!

♣ With some friends, see who can say this tongue-twister the most times in one minute – without getting in a muddle.

Peter Piper picked a peck of pickled pepper

A peck of pickled pepper Peter Piper picked

If Peter Piper picked a peck of pickled pepper

Where's the peck of pickled pepper

Peter Piper picked?

♣ Use the same rhythm **p**attern to make up your own **p** tongue-twister on the back of this sheet. For example:

Paula **P**ringle **p**lucked a **p**air of **p**urple **p**eaches.
A **p**air of **p**urple **p**eaches **P**aula **P**ringle **p**lucked... and so on

♣ Clap the rhythm till you're sure of it.

Teacher Timesavers: Spelling and language skills

Name_____

In English, **q** always brings its friend **u** with it.

❖ Read this story and use the words in the box to fill in the blanks.

The _____ was sitting _____ in bed, wrapped in her

_____ . A knock at the door made her Majesty _____

straighten up. 'Enter,' she cried. A _____ little gnome

ran into the room. 'Her Royal Highness Princess Megan has given

birth to _____ , five gorgeous little girls!' 'Bravo!' beamed

the Queen. 'Now leave me. I need peace and _____ to

enjoy this moment.' 'But, your Majesty, there is already a _____

of people at your door.' 'Silence! Never _____ my authority,'

interrupted the Queen, _____ with rage. The gnome was

_____ with fear, so the Queen relented and allowed her

subjects to enter and offer their congratulations.

question	queue
queen	quilt
quivering	quiet
quins	quaint
quaking	quietly
quickly	

Name _____

Many verbs begin with **re** in English.

♣ List as many as you can find.

Rr

recover   rehearse   revisit   rewrite

_____ _____ _____ _____

_____ _____ _____ _____

_____ _____ _____ _____

_____ _____ _____ _____

_____ _____ _____ _____

♣ What does **re** tell us in many of these words?

_____ _____ _____ _____

♣ Turn over this sheet and write about an incident you **re**member from when you were little.

_____ _____ _____ _____

Name_____

Ss

S is a friendly letter. It likes to blend with other consonants.

♣ List all the blends **s** makes with other consonants. Use the snake below to help you.

sc

♣ Now take one blend at a time and hunt for words. Who can collect the longest list?

sc: scab school Scotland

♣ **S**ometimes **s** makes a cluster with two other consonants, like this: **scr**. Are there any more?

♣ Turn over this **sh**eet and draw a big **sn**ake, decorate it in bright colours with **s** blends, then cut it out and hang it up.

| b | c | d | f | g | h | j | k | l | m | n | p | q | r | s | t | v | w | x | y | z |

Tt

Tt

❖ List all the songs you can find with a **t** word in the **t**itle or first line. Here are **t**wo to help you.

> Ten green bottles
>
> Twinkle, twinkle little star

❖ Make up your own song about something or someone beginning with **t**.

❖ With the help of your friends add some music using drums, cabasas, chime bars, maracas and other percussion instruments.

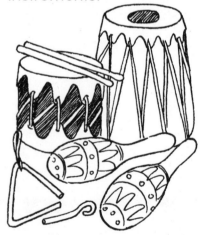

❖ When you're satisfied, **t**ape record it for your listening corner.

Un... just two letters, yet what a difference they can make.
They can change us from 'happy' to '**un**happy'.

♣ Hunt for words that begin with **un**
and see how many you can collect.

Uu

unable

unkind

unwelcome

♣ Turn over this sheet
and tell the story of the
unhappiest day of your
life – real or pretend!

Vv

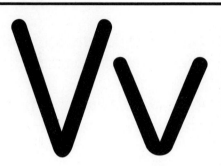

❖ List as many names starting with **V** as you can.

Varma

Vera

Victor

❖ Write a sentence about each one, using as many **v** words as possible.

Vera's voice was just like velvet.

_____

_____

_____

_____

_____

_____

_____

_____

❖ Put your sentences together to make a poem about your **v**ery special family.

❖ Edit it carefully, then display it.

❖ Publish a collection of **v** poems with your friends.

Welcome! Have fun playing consequences **w**ith a few friends. The trick is to **w**rite quickly.

✦ Cut out the two blank panels, then **w**rite the first **w**ord, fold back the paper and pass it on. Remember to concentrate on **w**ords starting with **w**.

Who?	Winston		
What?	whispered		
With whom?	to Wendy		
Where?	on the garden wall		
When?	on Whit Monday		
Why?	because he wanted to be her friend		

Name _____

Lots of words begin with **ex**.

✤ List some of them here.

Exeter
exciting
excuse me!

✤ Fill in the lost vowels in the words below.

f __ x   b __ x

f __ x   fl __ x

m __ x   t __ x __

c __ x   __ x __

__ x   __ x __ t

w __ x   t __ x __ c

t __ x

p __ x __ __

✤ Can you find some more?

Xx

EXTRA! **EX**TRA! READ ALL ABOUT IT!

✤ Write an article for a newspaper, using some words from your **ex** list, about a local crime.

Name_____

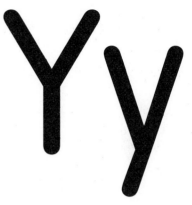

There's a virus in the computer! All the vowels (**a, e, i, o, u**) in the words beginning with **y** have disappeared. **Y**ou'll have to help!

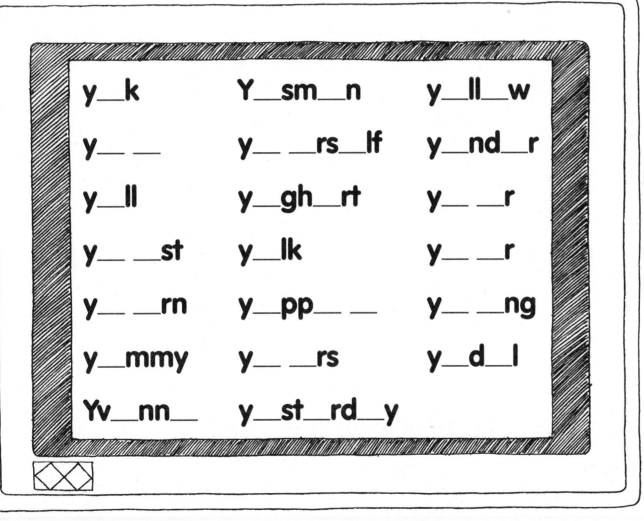

y__k   Y__sm__n   y__ll__w

y__ __   y__ __rs__lf   y__nd__r

y__ll   y__gh__rt   y__ __r

y__ __st   y__lk   y__ __r

y__ __rn   y__pp__ __   y__ __ng

y__mmy   y__ __rs   y__d__l

Yv__nn__   y__st__rd__y

❖ Turn over this sheet and write the words out in alphabetical order – ready to go back into the computer's word bank.

Name _____

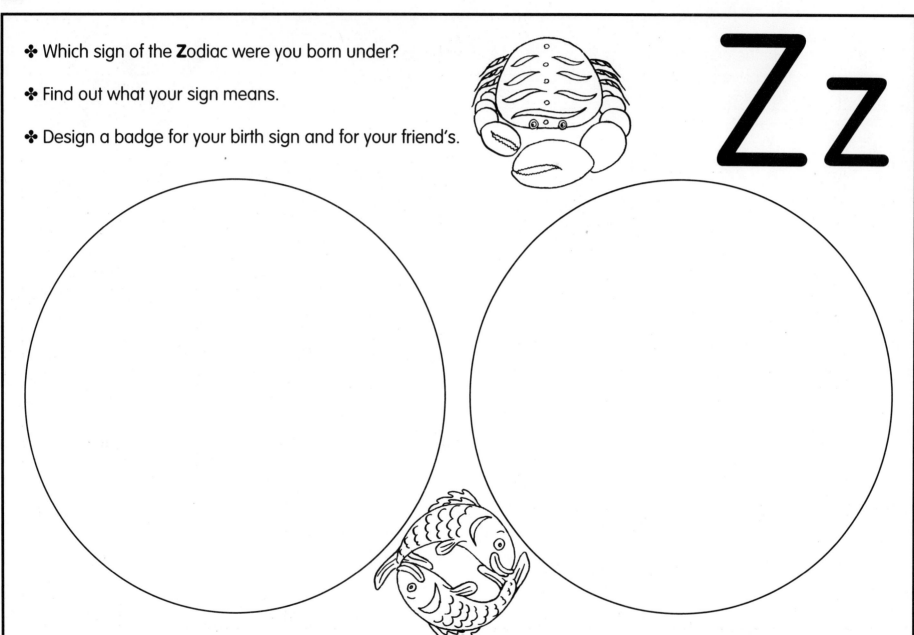

❖ Which sign of the **Z**odiac were you born under?

❖ Find out what your sign means.

❖ Design a badge for your birth sign and for your friend's.

Sh!

♣ Work quietly and make a picture dictionary using the words below.
Carry on over the page with more **sh** words if you like.

shadows	**shady**	**shampoo**	**shapes**	**shark**
sharp	**shave**	**sheep**	**sheet**	**shells**
shield	**shiny**	**ship**	**shirt**	**shoot**

ch

ch

♣ Provide the words for this page of a picture dictionary.
They all begin with **ch** of course!

This and that

♣ Solve **th**e clues to make your own collection of words starting with **th**.

- Never forget to say it: _ _ _ _ _   _ _ _

- You've got one on each hand: _ _ _ _ _ _

- It's very noisy in a storm: _ _ _ _ _ _ _

- Tom the piper's son was one: _ _ _ _ _ _

- These are sharp and prickly: _ _ _ _ _ _ _

- A small number: _ _ _ _ _ _

- Ten more than that: _ _ _ _ _ _ _ _

- It registers the temperature: _ _ _ _ _ _ _ _ _ _ _

- We use it when sewing: _ _ _ _ _ _ _

- We go here to watch plays: _ _ _ _ _ _ _ _

- A chair fit for a king: _ _ _ _ _ _ _

- A straw roof: _ _ _ _ _ _ _

♣ Turn the sheet over and make a picture dictionary. Make sure you put the words in alphabetical order.

wh

What can it be?

♣ Play 'I spy in my mind's eye something beginning with **wh**'.

| **1** It's golden. | **2** Farmers grow it. | **3** It goes to a mill. | **4** It's made into flour. |

wheat

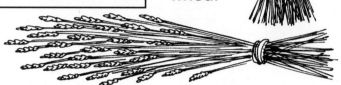

♣ Now make up four clues for each of the words below and see if your friends can guess them.

whale	whiskers	whisper	whirlpool
1	1	1	1
2	2	2	2
3	3	3	3
4	4	4	4

'Pick and mix' with r

A lot of words in English begin with **br**.

♣ Write down as many words beginning with **br** as you can in one minute.

brag   brave   brush

♣ Which other consonants have you seen blending with **r**? (There are six.) Write them below.

♣ Over the next few days, make a collection of words for each blend.

♣ Design a poster to keep **Br**itain **br**illiantly **br**ight and clean.

Blends with l

'Pick and mix' with l

Quite a lot of words in English begin with **bl**.

♣ Hunt them out and toss them into the **bl**anket!

blame

blue

blouse

blackboard

♣ Which other consonants blend with **l**? (There are five.)

♣ Make up some silly sentences using your **bl** words like the one below.

My **blue blouse blew** over the **bl**ackboard.

_____

_____

_____

Two of a kind?

♣ Cut out these consonants.

b	c	d
f	g	h
J	k	l
m	n	p
q	r	s
t	v	w
x	y	z

♣ Which vowels double up in English words? Cut them out.

aa	ee	ii	oo	uu

♣ Now follow the example shown below and try out the consonants one after another at the **beginning** and **end** of the double vowels. See how many words you can make. Don't forget blends with **r** and **l**.

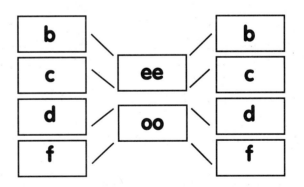

♣ Put your words to g**oo**d use and finish this story: 'D**ee**p in the w**oo**ds...'.

Name _____

ai

Take your partners!

Sometimes two vowels join together, like **ai**.

❖ List all the words you can find which have **ai** in them.

❖ Use some of your words to add more lines to the song, 'The r**ai**n in Sp**ai**n falls m**ai**nly on the pl**ai**n'. Here's an idea to help you get started.

The fair-haired pair just floated by on air.

_____

_____

_____

_____

_____

_____

❖ Which other vowels does **a** join up with?

Teacher Timesavers: Spelling and language skills

Authors' corner

Lots of words have **au** in them.

❧ Make a list of them here.

❧ Now is your chance to become an **au**thor, **lau**nching your first mystery story. Continue the story, using your **au** words. Here's how it all began:

Through no fault of his own, our audacious hero Paul

is caught in a trap in Australia..._____

_____

_____

_____

_____

_____

_____

❧ You can write further chapters on the back of this sheet.

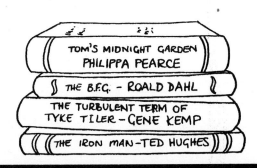

TOM'S MIDNIGHT GARDEN
PHILIPPA PEARCE

THE B.F.G. - ROALD DAHL

THE TURBULENT TERM OF
TYKE TILER - GENE KEMP

THE IRON MAN - TED HUGHES

Name _____

ea

Two heads are better than one

✣ Join a friend and hunt for words which have an **ea** pattern. Write them below. Here are some to get you going.

✣ Make up a limerick using some of the words from your collection. Here's an example for you to follow.

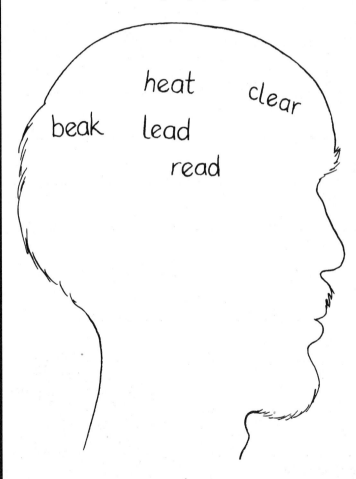

heat   clear

beak   lead

read

There was a young lady from D**ea**l
Who decided to have a large m**ea**l.
She ate a whole pike
Then fell off her bike
And said 'Oh, how dr**ea**dful I feel!'

_____

_____

_____

_____

✣ Find out which other vowels **e** joins up with.

Paddy's goat

♣ Work in a group of three. One of you should hunt for **oa** words, another should hunt for **oi** words and the third should hunt for **ou** words. Write them below.

♣ Now make up an hilari**ou**s tale about Paddy McGinty's g**oa**t. Take turns to write a sentence, using a word from y**ou**r own collection each time. The first sentence has been done to get y**ou** g**oi**ng.

Paddy McGinty had a beautiful sleek, black goat that got up to all kinds of tricks! _____

_____

_____

_____

_____

_____

_____

♣ See if you can find any **oe** words.

Name _____

ie

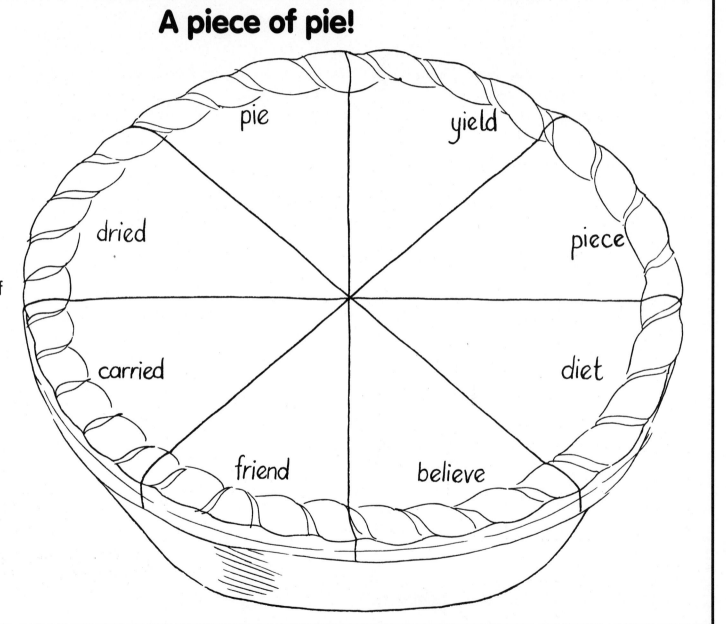

A piece of pie!

The letters **ie** are used together in a lot of English words.

♣ Hunt for other words which can be added to the p**ie**.

♣ Discuss with a fr**ie**nd why the words have been sorted out into these different p**ie**ces of the p**ie**, and write your words in the right p**ie**ces.

♣ Continue this story: 'I hurried over to my fr**ie**nd's house...'.

pie

yield

dried

piece

carried

diet

friend

believe

A quick quiz

? ?   ?   ?   ? ?   ?   ?

The letters **ui** are used frequently together.

❖ Have a q**ui**ck think about **ui** words that you know and then try the q**ui**z below.

• Someone who shows you round: _ _ _ _ _

• A feeling you have when you've done something wrong: _ _ _ _ _

• It goes nicely with a cup of tea: _ _ _ _ _ _ _

• A set of matching furniture: _ _ _ _ _

• A hectic chase: hot _ _ _ _ _ _ _

• They come out when you fall over: _ _ _ _ _ _ _

• A sailing holiday: _ _ _ _ _ _

• Schools, houses, offices and shops: _ _ _ _ _ _ _ _ _ _

• You might wear one on a special occasion: _ _ _ _

• A pleasant summer drink: _ _ _ _ _ _ _ _ _ _

Name _____

Vowel plus r

Getting together with r

Vowels enjoy getting together with **r**.

♣ Work against the clock. How long does it take you to collect 50 **ar** words?
St**ar**t now! Some have been done to help you.

1 syllable	2 syllables	3 syllables	4 syllables
cart	army	charity	harmonica

♣ Clap the rhythms that the words make.   ♣ Have a go at collecting the other pairs: **er, ir, or, ur**.

Getting together with w

Some v**ow**els like **a**, **e** and **o** often get together with **w**.
Here are some rhyming sentences that actors use to practise for parts that require a different accent from their **ow**n.

• H**ow** n**ow** br**ow**n c**ow**?
• Who s**aw** the jackd**aw** cl**aw** the str**aw**?
• Bring a n**ew** plate of st**ew** for Mr McGr**ew**.

❖ Make up some more sentences of your **ow**n using **aw**, **ew** and **ow** words and write them bel**ow**.

❖ Tape record yourself trying to say your sentences in the right accent for:
• 'Eastenders';
• 'Neighbours';
• 'The Six O'clock News';
• 'Brookside';
• 'Baywatch'.

_____

_____

_____

_____

_____

_____

_____

Name _____

Vowel plus y

Getting together with y

Y often likes to get together with the vowel **a**.

♣ Collect some **ay** words and write them below. Here are some to get you going

bray
crayfish
decay
say

♣ Now write a diary (real or pretend) about what you did last week. You must follow one special rule: every **day** has to include at least one **ay** word.

On Monday _____

On Tuesday _____

On Wednesday _____

On Thursday _____

On Friday _____

On Saturday _____

On Sunday _____

♣ Which other vowels does **y** like to join up with?

Holiday flight

✤ Get ready for your holiday fl**igh**t! Hunt for words which have the **igh** letter pattern and pack them into your overn**igh**t bag.

Sitting next to you on the plane are Mrs M**igh**t and Mr M**igh**t-Not and r**igh**t away they start to argue.

✤ Using your bag of words, write the account of this incident.

bright
mighty

_____

_____

_____

_____

_____

_____

_____

_____

_____

Name _____

-ough

WPC Clough in action

Written below are some extracts from WPC Cl**ough**'s diary, after she was called to the scene of an accident.

❧ Supply the vital missing words. (CLUE: they all contain the letter pattern **ough**.)

❧ Brainstorm all the words you can think of with **ough** in them first to help you.

Question 1 Have you always lived in _____ , madam?

Question 2 Which _____ was it exactly that the cradle fell from?

Question 3 Was there not a _____ branch to put the cradle on?

Question 4 The neighbours tell me they heard the baby _____ and spluttering just before the incident. Is that so?

Question 5 Do you now believe you _____ to have stayed outside near the baby?

Question 6 Had the field been _____ recently? Yes? What a good job or the baby would have had a very _____ landing.

Well, that's _____ for now, thank you, madam. Make sure you take more care in future.

❧ Have you guessed which nursery rhyme this was based on?

❧ Choose a favourite rhyme and a different letter pattern and set up a similar interview to try out on a friend.

Split personality

In words such as **y**ou, **y**es and **y**ellow, **y** is used like a consonant. However, **y** can also be a vowel, for example in happ**y**, mumm**y** and loll**y**, and in places where we might expect an **i** to be.

♣ The word processor has lost the **y** and the **s** from all the words below. Supply these missing letters, then sort the words into alphabetical order.

cr___ ___ tal   ___ ___ mpath___   m___ ___ ter ___

ab___ ___ ___   ox ___gen   h ___ mn

m___th   ___ ___ rup   ___ ___ ___ tem

___ ___ llabu ___   ph ___ ___ ic ___   t ___ pical

___ ___ mbol   ___ ___ camore   c ___ gnet

p___ramid   h ___ pnoti ___t   ___ ___ mmetr ___

♣ Discuss with a friend what all these words mean. Remember to check in a dictionary if you're not sure.

♣ See if you can find any more words which use **y** instead of **i**.

Name _____

Soft c

Spot the difference

✤ Read these two sentences aloud.
- The **c**old **c**ountry **c**ats **c**uddled up to keep warm.
- In the **c**ity, **C**yril made **c**ertain the **c**ircus stalls had **c**entral heating.

✤ Explain the difference between the **c**s in the two sentences.

_____

_____

✤ Look **c**arefully again. Which vowels follow the **c**s in the first sentence?
Which ones follow the **c**s in the second sentence?

✤ Collect as many words which have a soft **c** (like an 's' sound) as you can and use them to write a modern version of the **C**inderella story for a new **c**inema production.

_____

_____

_____

_____

✤ Tomorrow check **g** and compare your findings with **c**.

Silent letters

Some letters keep quiet and don't make a sound.

✤ Pick out the silent letter from the words below and **w**rite them in the boxes. Add as many words to each set as you can. A dictionary will help. You can't add a word till you **k**now what it means. (Dictionaries can help there too!)

calm walk	honest rhino	gnash	scent	pneumonia	debt lamb	guard	write

✤ Write down any other silent letters you can think of.

Name _____

Abbreviations

Popular abbreviations

❖ Hunt for words to add to these lists.

❖ Discuss with a friend what they all stand for.

People	Places	Towns	Counties	Days	Months	Names
Mr	St	L'pool	Berks	Mon	Jan	Meg
Col	Sq	N'castle	Lancs			Teddy

❖ On the back of this sheet, draft a short story using some abbreviations from your lists.
You could include some of your own inventions such as **chn** (children) or **pol** (police).

More abbreviations

Some abbreviations are sets of initials which stand for words.

✣ Write down what the abbreviations below stand for and add any others you know.

BC _____   NB _____

AD _____   PS _____

a.m. _____   PTO _____

p.m. _____   RIP _____

AWOL _____   RSVP _____

BBC _____   SAE _____

COD _____   UK _____

EC _____   UN _____

HRH _____   USA _____

HM _____   VIP _____

IOU _____   _____

ITV _____

✣ Make up some more abbreviations that are special to your school or community.

✣ Ask your friends to work them out.

Name _____

Plurals

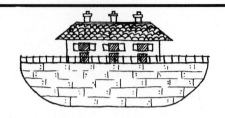

Two by two

♣ Look at the pictures on the left. There is only one of everything. Help Noah to check his list to make sure he takes two of everything.

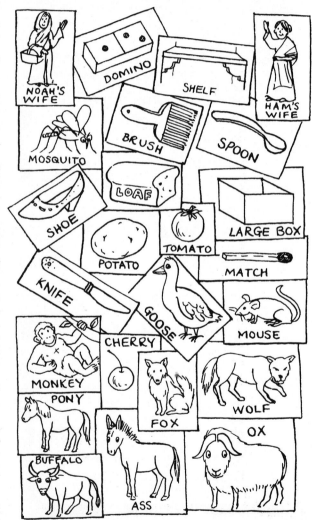

NOAH'S WIFE
DOMINO
SHELF
HAM'S WIFE
MOSQUITO
BRUSH
SPOON
LOAF
SHOE
LARGE BOX
TOMATO
POTATO
MATCH
KNIFE
GOOSE
MOUSE
CHERRY
MONKEY
PONY
FOX
WOLF
BUFFALO
OX
ASS

2 **a** _ _ _ _ _ _ _

2 **b** _ _ _ _ _ _ _ _

2 **f** _ _ _ _ _

2 **m** _ _ _ _ _ _ _

2 **m** _ _ _ _ _ _ _ _

2 **w** _ _ _ _

2 **p** _ _ _ _ _ _

2 **w** _ _ _ _ _ _

2 **o** _ _

2 **m** _ _ _ _

2 **g** _ _ _ _

a bag of **c** _ _ _ _ _ _

a box of **m** _ _ _ _ _ _ _ _

2 large **b** _ _ _ _ _

2 **k** _ _ _ _ _ _

2 **s** _ _ _ _ _

2 **l** _ _ _ _ _

2 kilos of **p** _ _ _ _ _ _ _

2 kilos of **t** _ _ _ _ _ _ _ _

2 pairs of **s** _ _ _ _ _

2 sets of **b** _ _ _ _ _ _

2 sets of **d** _ _ _ _ _ _ _

2 **s** _ _ _ _ _ _

♣ List the things you would take on the ark. You only have a small case. Justify your choice to a friend.

Name _____

Compound nouns

English is full of compound nouns – that's when two nouns join up to make one new one.

♣ Work through the alphabet collecting as many compound nouns as you can.

Afternoon	N
Bedtime	O
Cheesecake	P
D	Q
E	R
F	S
G	**Teapot**
Handbag	U
I	V
J	W
K	X
L	Y
Moonlight	Z

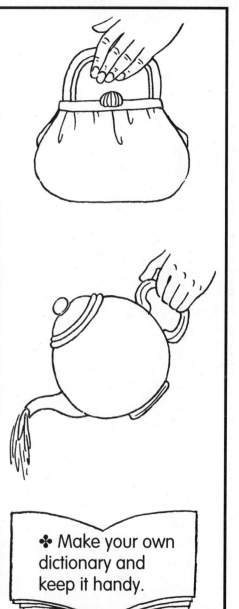

♣ Make your own dictionary and keep it handy.

Name _____

Doublets

Two for the price of one!

❖ Read the rhymes below.

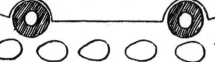

My old man said follow the van
and don't dilly-dally on the way.

Higgledy-piggledy my black hen
She lays eggs for gentlemen.

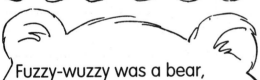

Fuzzy-wuzzy was a bear,
Fuzzy-wuzzy had no hair,
Fuzzy-wuzzy wasn't fuzzy-wuzzy,
Was he?

❖ Did you spot the unusual words? These words have been made by adding a second word that's almost the same as the first.

♣ Guess what these words mean.

tittle-tattle: hotchpotch:

shilly-shally: mishmash:

❖ Check in a dictionary to see if you were right.

❖ Here's a few more to puzzle out:

1    2    3

_____   _____   _____

New for old

Sometimes we put parts of two words together to make a brand-new word, for example **international** and **police** are combined to make **Interpol**, and **news** and **broadcaster** make **newscaster**.

❧ Which new words came from these pairs?

- helicopter and port → _____

- channel and tunnel → _____

- Oxford and Cambridge → _____

- motor and hotel → _____

- breakfast and lunch → _____

- cheese and hamburger → _____

- smoke and fog → _____

- gigantic and enormous → _____

- mist and drizzle → _____

- orange and lemonade → _____

❧ Make up some new words of your own.

_____ + _____ → _____

_____ + _____ → _____

_____ + _____ → _____

_____ + _____ → _____

_____ + _____ → _____

_____ + _____ → _____

_____ + _____ → _____

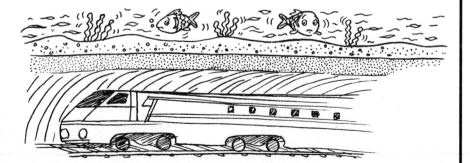

Name _____

-ful

A spoonful of sugar

Have you noticed that **-ful** comes in very handy for telling us how much of something we need?

✤ Work out the quantities shown in the illustrations below. The first one has been done for you.

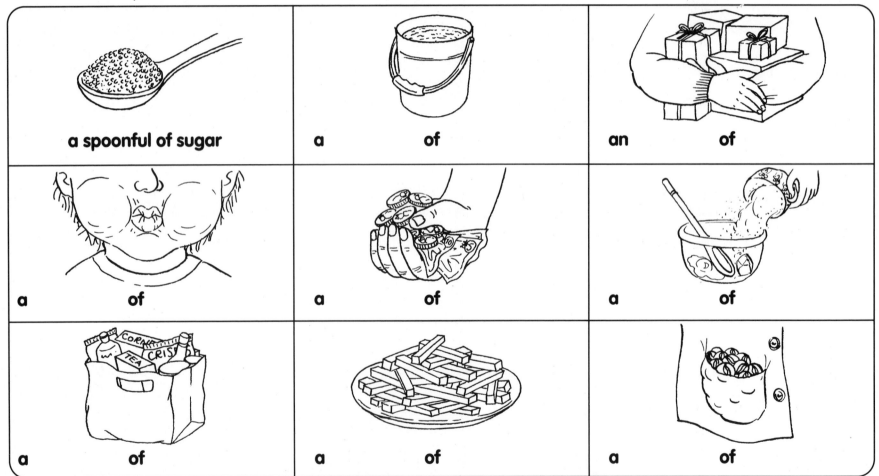

a spoonful of sugar	a _____ of _____	an _____ of _____
a _____ of _____	a _____ of _____	a _____ of _____
a _____ of _____	a _____ of _____	a _____ of _____

✤ Make up some unusual recipes using these quantities.

Small but powerful!

Just the two letters **er** can change **do** to **doer**, an **action** into a **person** and a **verb** into a **noun**.

❖ Set to work on the lists below. Look carefully! Sometimes there's a little trick to watch out for.

buy → buyer	bake → baker	run → runner	fly → flier
do → doer			
eat → eater			

❖ Talk to your friends about those little tricks.
❖ Turn over this sheet and write a story about the 'baker's dozen'.

Name _____

-ness

Loch Ness Nessy!

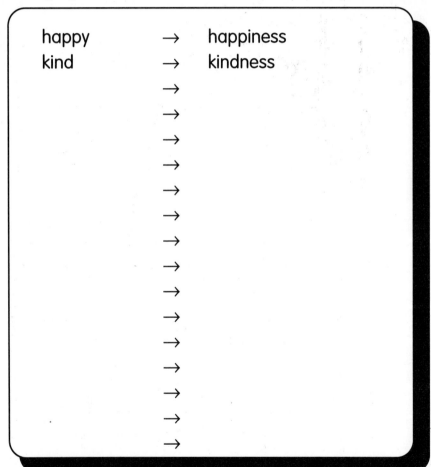

Nessy knows you can turn adjectives into nouns just by using **-ness**!

✤ Can you finish Nessy's list by adding your own adjectives and changing them into nouns. Watch out for adjectives that end in **y**.

happy	→	happiness
kind	→	kindness
	→	
	→	
	→	
	→	
	→	
	→	
	→	
	→	
	→	
	→	
	→	
	→	
	→	
	→	

✤ Write a song about how Nessy feels all on her own at the bottom of the loch.

All together now!

-tion is a popular ending for nouns. Here are some rhythmical ones that sound great when you clap as you chant them together.

affectation   aggravation   elation   fabrication   habitation   inspiration   jubilation   location
meditation   navigation   observation   privatisation   quotation   unification   visitation

♣ Check what the words mean in a dictionary.

♣ Arrange some of the words in any order to make four verses of a rhythm and sound poem.

♣ Add percussion to your chant and record it when you're satisfied with it.

-ment, -ation

Abracadabra!

Often a verb can be changed into a noun by adding **-ment** or **-ation** on to the end.

❖ Look at this list of verbs and change them to nouns.
❖ Write each noun in the right balloon.

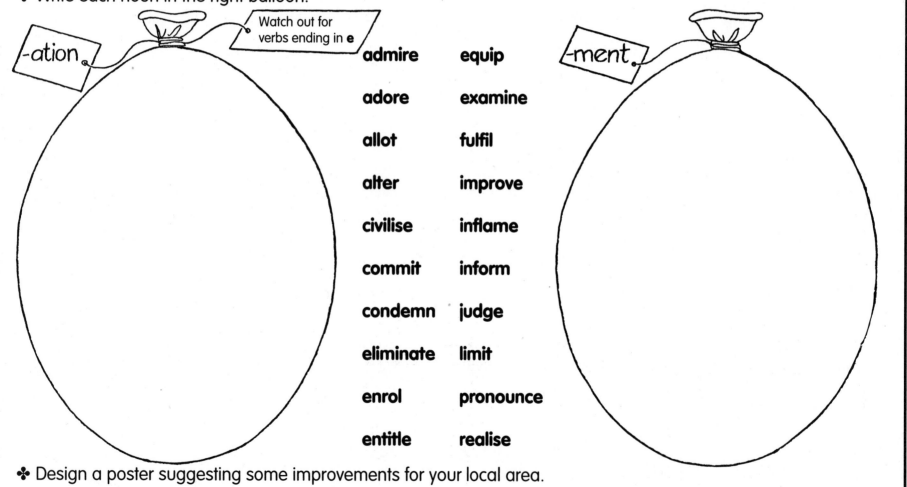

Watch out for verbs ending in **e**

-ation

-ment

admire	equip
adore	examine
allot	fulfil
alter	improve
civilise	inflame
commit	inform
condemn	judge
eliminate	limit
enrol	pronounce
entitle	realise

❖ Design a poster suggesting some improvements for your local area.

Popularity poll

-our is quite a common ending for nouns in English.

♣ Hunt for some nouns ending in **-our** and write them in the suit of arm**our**.

♣ Nice rum**our**s are circulating about y**our** new neighb**our**s. Use y**our** **-our** words to write down what people are saying about them.

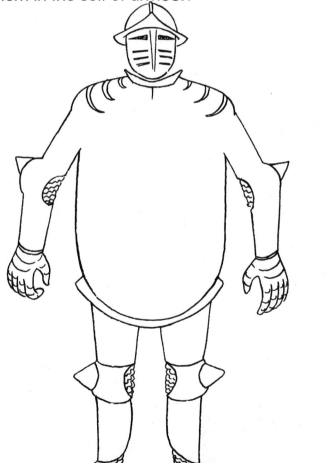

Name _____

-ence, -ory

Question time

♣ Write down as many nouns as you can ending with **-ence**. You will then be ready to play 'Question time'.

audience
confidence
sentence

• Secretly choose one word from your list.
• Ask your friends to guess the word by asking you questions. They can only ask questions that have a yes or no answer. For example: 'Is it a feeling?', 'Is it an event?', and so on.
• Limit the number of questions or set a time limit. You can award points too if you want to.

♣ You can also play this game with other word patterns. Try **-ory** words next time:
factory;
dormitory;
observatory....

All change!

❖ Change these verbs to nouns. (Helpful hint: they all end in **-sion**.)
❖ Write an explanation of what each word means.

Verbs	Nouns	Your definition
collide	collision	_____
conclude	_____	_____
confuse	_____	_____
decide	_____	_____
erode	_____	_____
exclude	_____	_____
explode	_____	_____
fuse	_____	_____
include	_____	_____
intrude	_____	_____
provide	_____	_____
revise	_____	_____

❖ Check your definitions in a dictionary to see if you were right.

Professor Proctor to the rescue!

✤ Profess**or** Proct**or** knows all the answers. Do you? Write down what all these people do. If you're not sure, check in a dictionary.

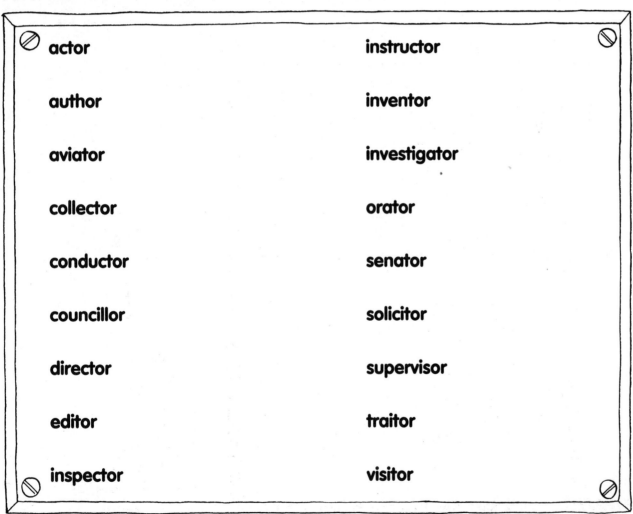

actor	instructor
author	inventor
aviator	investigator
collector	orator
conductor	senator
councillor	solicitor
director	supervisor
editor	traitor
inspector	visitor

✤ Imagine that you are one of these people. On the back of this sheet write a diary entry for a day in your life.

Opposites

There are lots of prefixes you can put at the front of words to change them into their opposites. There's **in-** and **im-** and **ir-** and **il-**.

♣ Which prefix would fit these words?

accurate

capable

considerate

credible

dependent

direct

legal

logical

polite

possible

probable

regular

♣ Oh dear, all these words have been mixed up. It's up to you to put them right.

irmobile

imattentive

imcorrect

iladequate

unfinite

inperfect

irexpensive

ilresponsible

imconvenient

uncomplete

♣ **in-** is probably the most popular prefix. List as many **in-** words as you can.

Name _____

-ful, -less

On the contrary

One way of saying the opposite in English is by changing the suffix at the end of adjectives from **-ful** to **-less**. This way care**ful** becomes care**less**. You have to take care, though, as it doesn't work every time – have you ever come across forget**less**?

✤ Hunt through the alphabet and see how many opposites you can find.

A	**J**	**S**
B	**K**	**T**
Careful/careless	**L**	**U**
D	**M**	**V**
E	**N**	**W**
F	**O**	**X**
G	**P**	**Y**
Helpful/	**Q**	**Z**
I	**Restful/**	

✤ Use your words to describe a famous person.

Changing jobs

Did you know that we are **able** to change verbs into adjectives?

✤ Use **able** to change these verbs to adjectives, then put them into the collecting bags.

change	accept	believe	compel	envy
manage	comfort	love	control	pity
notice	enjoy	move	forget	rely
service	laugh	use	regret	vary

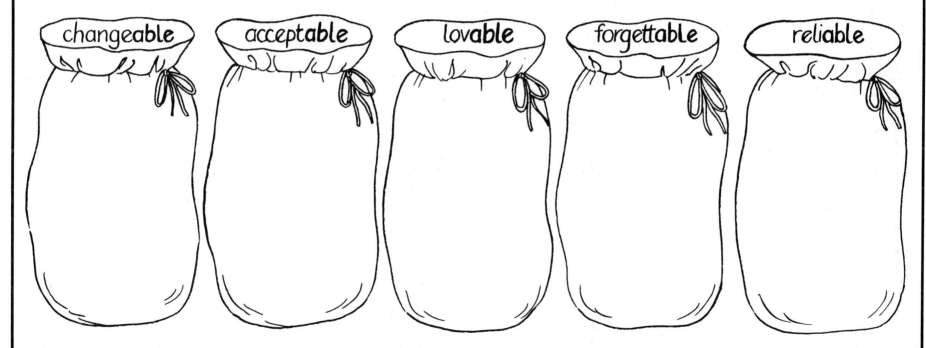

changeable   acceptable   lovable   forgettable   reliable

✤ Discuss with a friend the differences between the five bags of words.
✤ Use your adjectives to describe someone in your class. See if your friends can guess who it is.

-OUS

Changes, changes!

It's easy to change nouns into adjectives with the help of the suffix **-ous**. For example, courage becomes courage**ous**. Sometimes you have to make a little change, for example grac**e** becomes grac**ious**.

❖ Turn these nouns into adjectives and add some of your own.

nerve →

outrage →

danger →

joy →

venom →

space →

injury →

♣ Make up a dictionary entry for each adjective below.

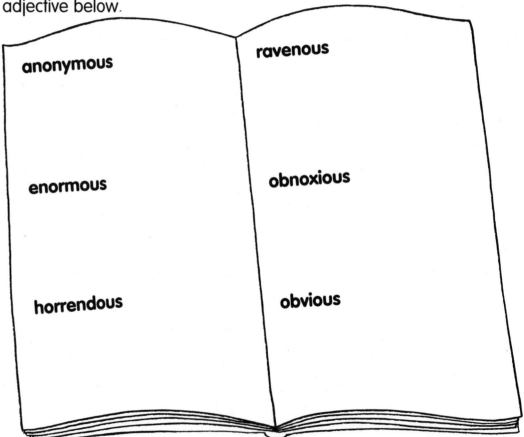

anonymous

enormous

horrendous

ravenous

obnoxious

obvious

❖ Start a collection of jokes for a 'humor**ous** corner' in your classroom.

Name _____

Use your logic

♣ On the back of this sheet brainstorm adjectives ending in **-ic**.

♣ Write them out in alphabetical order here with an explanation of what each one means.

acrobatic: _____

atomic: _____

automatic: _____

_____

_____

_____

_____

_____

_____

_____

_____

♣ Work with a few friends. Take it in turns to read out one of your definitions. See who can get the most words right.

-ical

Thinking caps on

♣ Solve these clues and find the adjectives. (Helpful hint: all the adjectives end in **-ical**.)

• The order of the letters: _____

• Things that make us laugh: _____

• A check up at the doctor's: _____

• The way actors might behave: _____

• To do with the eyes: _____

• Upright: _____

• Hot and humid: _____

• Connected with the government: _____

• Done with the wave of a wand: _____

• You can't tell the difference: _____

DAILY NEWS

LOGICAL LIBRARIAN LEADS WAY

♣ Write a headline for a **topical** piece of news and a front page article to go with it.

Spot the pattern

♣ Look carefully at this list of adjectives. What have they all got in common?

audible	unintelligible
inaudible	legible
credible	illegible
incredible	permissible
compatible	possible
incompatible	impossible
comprehensible	responsible
incomprehensible	irresponsible
divisible	terrible
indivisible	invincible
horrible	visible
intelligible	invisible

♣ Use as many of these words as you can to retell a heroic tale from the past such as David and Goliath, Boudicca, the Rani of Jhansi or Mary Seacole:

_____

_____

_____

_____

_____

_____

_____

_____

_____

_____

_____

♣ Use your dictionary to check the meaning of any words you are unsure about.

Name _____

-en

Widen your horizons

❖ Add to this list of adjectives that will join up with **en** to make verbs.

wide	→	widen
soft	→	soften
	→	
	→	
	→	
	→	
	→	
	→	
	→	

❖ Use your verbs to write instructions that offer good advice, for example:

Do quieten down so you don't wake the baby!

_____

_____

_____

_____

_____

_____

_____

_____

❖ **en-** works as a prefix at the start of words too, like **en**large. Use a dictionary to find some more.

Energise your writing

❖ Change these nouns and adjectives into verbs by using the suffix **-ise**.

advert → advertise	**formal** →	**popular** →
author →	**individual** →	**private** →
civil →	**idol** →	**real** →
critic →	**legal** →	**regular** →
drama →	**marginal** →	**vandal** →
equal →	**monopoly** →	**victim** →
final →	**national** →	

❖ Use these words to create rhythmical, clapping poems that you can chant with your friends, like the example below.

Don't vandalise

Don't victimise

Don't marginalise

Just equalise.

_____ _____

_____ _____

_____ _____

_____ _____

❖ Perform them for other classes, using percussion instruments if you wish.

Name _____

-ow, -ew, -aw

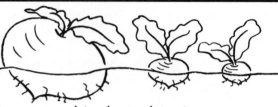

Making connections

Do you remember the story of the enormous turnip – gr**ow**ing and gr**ow**ing till it gr**ew** so big that when it was fully gr**ow**n no-one could pull it up?

The modern word gr**ow** comes to us from the Old English word 'gr**ow**an'. Other words are similar, for example, there's bl**ow** from bl**ow**an; dr**aw** from dr**aw**en; thr**ow** from thr**aw**an and kn**ow** from cn**aw**an.

♣ Write four very short stories, like the turnip one above, based on the words: bl**ow**, dr**aw**, thr**ow** and kn**ow**.

1

_____

_____

_____

_____

2

_____

_____

_____

_____

3

_____

_____

_____

_____

4

_____

_____

_____

_____

Apostrophes

For informal pieces of writing, we often abbreviate. This means that words are shortened by popping in an apostrophe (') to show that there's a letter missing.

It's always happening to:

is	–	's

— How's that!
— Who's there?
— What's it like?

and to

are	–	're

— They're off!
— We're late!
— You're kidding!

and to

not	–	n't

— I haven't – I mustn't
— I can't – I oughtn't
— I don't – I didn't
— I daren't – I shouldn't
— I won't – I couldn't
— I mightn't – I wouldn't

✤ Use some of these to write a humorous poem about yourself.

In trouble again!

Name _____

Double consonants

Doubling up

The two suffixes **-ing** and **-ed** are often used at the end of verbs.
They tell us what's happen**ing** today and what happen**ed** yesterday.
Sometimes when you add **-ing** or **-ed** to a word something doubles up.

❧ Look carefully at the words in the balloons. Add other words that have the same doubling up trick!

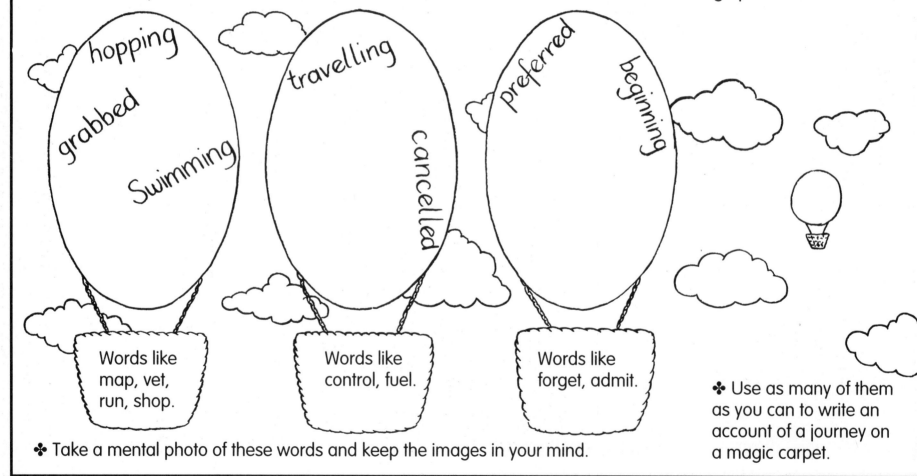

hopping
grabbed
Swimming

travelling
cancelled

preferred
beginning

Words like map, vet, run, shop.

Words like control, fuel.

Words like forget, admit.

❧ Use as many of them as you can to write an account of a journey on a magic carpet.

❧ Take a mental photo of these words and keep the images in your mind.

Name _____

Happy families

♣ Look at the verbs below and then hunt for their relatives among the nouns, adjectives and adverbs. Remember to think about prefixes and suffixes.

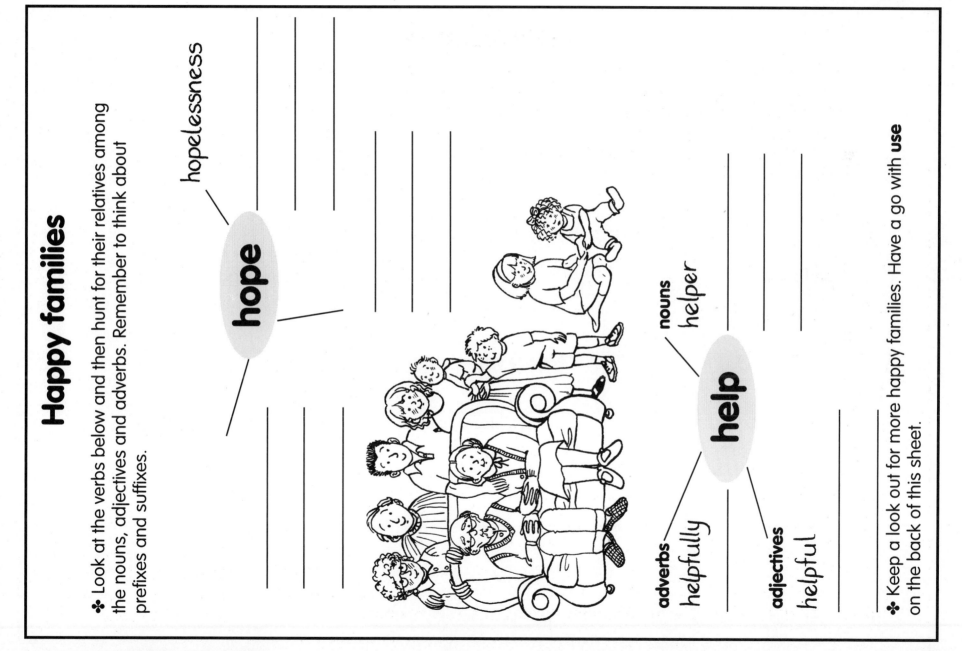

hopelessness

hope

help

nouns
helper

adverbs
helpfully

adjectives
helpful

♣ Keep a look out for more happy families. Have a go with **use** on the back of this sheet.

Name _____

Close relations

Close relations

Signus is the Latin word for mark and gives us the English word **sign**.

♣ Work out what all the close relations of **sign** that are written below might mean.
Check in a dictionary if you get stuck.

♣ Write the meanings in your own words.

assign:

_____

ensign: **resign:**

_____   _____

signature: **resignation:**

_____   _____

signet ring: **consignment:**

_____   ┌─────────────────┐   _____
                                 │ Read the signs!│
signal: └─────────────────┘   **design:**

_____   _____

signpost: **designate:**

_____   _____

                         designer: **insignia:**

_____   _____

Always look for close relations as similar meanings mean similar spellings!

Hieroglyphics

This is the script the Ancient Egyptians used.

a	**y**	**a**	**w**
b	**p**	**f**	**m**
n	**r**	**h**	**h**
kh	**<u>h</u>**	**s**	*s*
k	**k**	**g**	**t**
<u>t</u>	**d**	**<u>d</u>**	**l**

✤ How does it differ from the English alphabet?

✤ How many symbols are there?

✤ Invent a symbol to represent each English letter that is missing from this script.

✤ Using hieroglyphics, sketch some notices for your classroom.

Cyrillic script

Cyrillic script

In different parts of the world, people write in different scripts. Here is the Cyrillic alphabet which is used in Russia. English sounds are written underneath to help you.

Russian	а	в	б	г	д	е	ё	ж	з	и	й	к	л	м	н	о	п	р	с	т	у
English	a	b	v	g	dye	yo	j	z	i	ee	k	l	m	n	o	p	r	s	t	oo	

Russian	ф	х	ц	ч	ш	щ	ы	э	ю	я
English	f	h	ts	ch	sh	shch	oi	e	you	ya

❖ Leap into your James Bond shoes and decode this secret message.

Кан чо мйт мэ ин Лондон томоppo

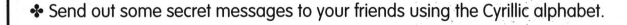

_____

❖ Send out some secret messages to your friends using the Cyrillic alphabet.

Chinese characters

The two best known languages of China are Mandarin and Cantonese. Both languages use characters for writing instead of letters. The Chinese write with brushes as they value writing as a form of art. Characters started out rather like pictures as you can see below:

gate

door

mountain

field

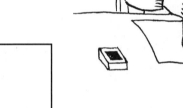

♣ Have a go at writing these characters. Use a fine brush and black ink or paint.

♣ Now try these

mouth

tongue

ox

horse

♣ Find out more from your school or local library about Chinese writing and painting and try them out in class.

Name _____

Counting to ten

Counting to ten

♣ Practise writing 1 to 10 in different ways.

Panjabi numerals	੧	੨	੩	੪	੫	੬	੭	੮	੯	੧੦	
Start here →											End here
Urdu numerals	۱	۹	۸	۷	۶	۵	۴	۳	۲	۱	
End here											**← Start here**
Roman numerals	I	II	III	IV	V	VI	VII	VIII	IX	X	
Start here →											End here

♣ Find out how to count to 10 in different languages.

North Indian	Swahili	French	German	Italian	Russian	
ik	moja				odeen	
doh	mbili				dva	
teen	tatu				tree	
char	nne				cheteeray	
panj	tano				piat	
che	sita				shest	
satt	saba				siem	
ath	nane				vosiem	
nau	tisa				dieyviet	
das	kumi				dieysiet	

Oodles of money

♣ Match the currency to the country.

Bangladesh	1 lira/100 centesimi
China	1 rouble/100 kopeks
France	1 taka/100 paise
Germany	1 shilling/100 cents
Greece	1 dollar/100 cents
India/Pakistan	1 yuan/100 fen
Israel	1 franc/100 centimes
Italy	1 escudo/100 centavos
Japan	1 drachma/100 lepta
Kenya/Uganda	1 shekel/100 agorot
Norway	1 peseta/100 centimos
Portugal	1 yen/100 sen
Russia/Ukraine	1 mark/100 pfennigs
Spain	1 rupee/100 paise
United States of America	1 krona/100 öre

♣ Design some banknotes and coins for a new country in outer space.

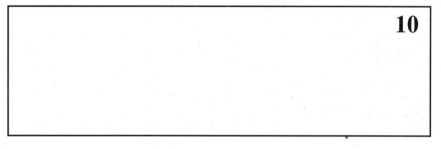

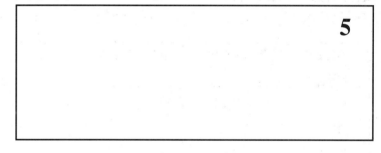

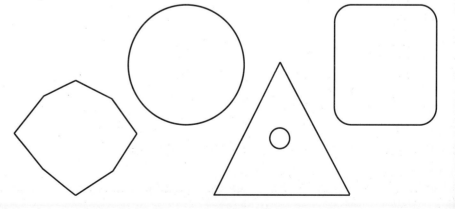

Greetings

Greetings

♣ Write down all the different ways you can greet people.
Add more speech bubbles if you need them.

HEY UP!

HOW DO.

HI!

HELLO!

♣ Discuss with a friend which greetings you might use for your teacher; your parents; your friends; strangers.

♣ Make them into a large frieze for your classroom.

♣ How many different ways can you find to say goodbye?

Water water everywhere

♣ Match each word for water to the language by colouring both raindrops the same colour.

♣ Add some more raindrops with words from your local area or home language or places you've been to on holiday.

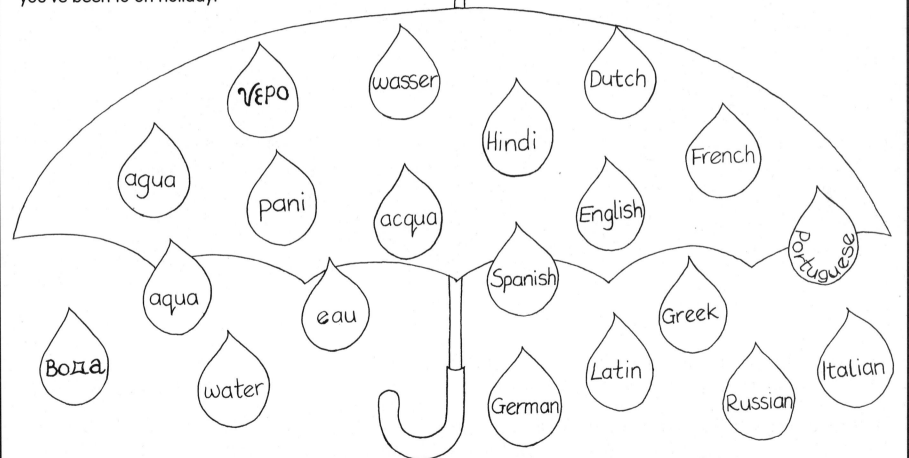

♣ Make up a similar game for your friends based on words for **river** or **waterfall** or **it's raining**.

Language survey

Name _____

Language survey

❖ Find out from everyone in your group which languages they know and complete the chart.

Name	Languages I understand	Speak	Read	Write

❖ List on the back of this sheet all the advantages of being bilingual.

❖ Write down where everyone learned these languages and who they speak them with.

❖ Continue your survey round the class, then you can display the results on a map of the world on the wall for all to see.

Different dialects

✤ Translate these Geordie expressions into standard English and into the way people would say them where you live.

Geordie	Standard English	Your local dialect
Me mam'll play war with us.		
Give owr.		
Divn't de that.		
There's wor kid.		
A'll get wrong off me mam.		
A divn't na.		
Why ay, canny lass.		
Had away and be ganing.		
Yer me best marra.		

✤ Discuss with a friend the different ways you might talk with different people or on different occasions.

Think of: **places** – at home/in class/in the playground/on holiday/at the doctor's...

people – friends/parents/grandparents/teachers/headteacher/ police/TV interview...

feelings – relaxed/nervous/angry/worried/sad/in trouble....

✤ Write about your findings.

Proverbs

Name _____

Proverbs

Grannies from the Caribbean are often full of good advice for their grandchildren.

♣ Write these Creole proverbs out in standard English.

• 'Dih older dih violin,
de sweeter de tune.'

_____
_____

• 'Hurry hurry mek bad curry.'

_____

• 'When de farmer away,
Jackass take holiday.'

_____
_____

• 'Better don't count de
chickens before dey hatch.'

_____
_____

• 'Don' never hang yuh hat
higher dan yuh can reach.'

_____
_____

• 'Who de cap fit
let dem wear it.'

_____
_____

♣ Discuss with a friend
what advice these
proverbs are actually
giving.

♣ Make a collection of
useful proverbs for your
class.

96

Accentuate the positive

Some people think you're common or stupid or a troublemaker if you don't talk posh. That's not fair, is it? You can still be a nice person.

♣ Talk to your friends about this 10-year-old's view, then make a list of all the good points about local dialects and accents.

_____

_____

_____

_____

_____

_____

_____

_____

♣ Draft a letter to your local newspaper about your views and find out what other readers think.

Language change

Name _____

A changing language

❖ Look carefully at these lines from 'The Wife of Bath's Tale' written by Geoffrey Chaucer:

> I grante thee lyf, if thou kanst tellen me
> What thing is it that wommen moost desiren.
> Be war, and keep thy nekke-boon from iren!
> And if thou kanst nat tellen it anon,
> Yet wol I yeve thee leve for to gon
> A twelf-month and a day, to seche and leere
> An answere suffisant in this mateere;
> And suretee wol I han, er that thou pace,
> Thy body for to yelden in this place.
>
> This is what English was like 600 years ago! It has changed a lot since then and it keeps on changing all the time as we need new words and phrases for new situations.
>
> ❖ Discuss Chaucer's English with a friend. What words do you recognise? How would we spell them today?
>
> ❖ See if you can work out what Chaucer is saying.

❖ Here are some words our great grandparents used frequently. What would we use today?

wireless →

gramophone →

petticoat →

stove →

gas mantle →

closet →

long johns →

toasting fork →

jerry →

drawers →

❖ Make a list of words we use today that our great grandparents would not have heard when they were young.

computer

astronaut

_____

_____

_____

_____

_____

_____

_____

Long, long ago

Settlers to Britain brought their languages with them and influenced the rich development of English over the centuries.

♣ Look at the different groups opposite and then at the words below. Work out which group brought which words and write them in the right boxes.

♣ Check your answers in a dictionary.
♣ Try to find out more about these settlers.

Celts were the earliest inhabitants of Britain.

Romans came to Britain in AD43.

Over 1000 years ago **Vikings** came to Britain.

Greek influence first came to Britain via the Romans.

album	consul	fellow	idea	myth	tweed
axis	coracle	forum	idiot	orchestra	want
bairn	crisis	genius	January	rostrum	whisky
bog	crooked	glen	knife	saga	wrong
circus	cycle	gymnasium	loch	skin	
chorus	delta	hit	macintosh	street	
clan	exit	husband	miser	take	

Words from names

The heroes of Greece and Rome

❖ Find out about the important figures in the list below and write down the English words that come from their names. Make sure you know what the words mean.

Ceres: _____

Echo: _____

Electra: _____

Hercules: _____

Hero: _____

Janus: _____

Luna: _____

Mars: _____

Pan: _____

Pluto: _____

The Muses: _____

The Titans: _____

Vulcan: _____

❖ Read all the myths about the exciting adventures of the Greek and Roman gods.

❖ Retell your favourite one in your own words.

Name _____

  # Number puzzles

unum means one in Latin.	**bi** means two.	**tri** means three.	**decem** means ten.
♣ Discuss with a friend what these words mean: unique uniform unit unisex union unicorn united unicycle unify universal ♣ Check in your dictionary to see if you were right.	♣ Can you add to this list? bilingual bigamist ♣ Check in your dictionary to make sure you know what all the words mean.	♣ Solve the clues to find words beginning **tri-** that mean the following: a three-sided figure a three-wheeled bike a three-legged stand a three-coloured flag a three-pronged fork a three-people band a million, million, million three children born together	♣ See how many words beginning with **dec-** you can find. Take care – you want only those connected with ten! December ♣ On the back of this sheet write one calendar entry for each month of the year using a word from these lists every time.

Name _____

cent-

Hundreds and hundreds

Centum is the Latin word for 'hundred'. There are many words in English which have the pattern **cent** in them.
♣ Unscramble the words below and try to work out if they've been given the right meaning! (Use a dictionary to help you.)

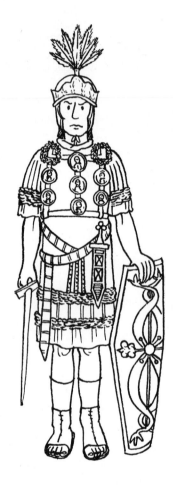

tnecrep = _ _ _ _ _ _ _ : one part in a hundred

ionturnec = _ _ _ _ _ _ _ _ _ : French coins

smitecen = _ _ _ _ _ _ _ _ : Roman soldier in charge of 100 men

trynuce = _ _ _ _ _ _ _ : a hundred years

timenercet = _ _ _ _ _ _ _ _ _ : a minibeast

yrantence = _ _ _ _ _ _ _ _ : a measurement of length

biliancennet = _ _ _ _ _ _ _ _ _ _ _ : a measurement of liquid

edragenict = _ _ _ _ _ _ _ _ _ : a 100th anniversary

detinecpe = _ _ _ _ _ _ _ _ _ : measure of temperature

rittlenice = _ _ _ _ _ _ _ _ _ : 200 years anniversary celebration

♣ Add on the back of this sheet any more words you can think of which have the **cent** pattern.

Name _____

Ancient inheritance

♣ Hunt for words with the prefixes, **anti-**, **inter-**, **sub-**, **super-** and **trans**. These have come to us from Greece and Rome.

anti- (against)	**inter-** (between)	**sub-** (under)	**super-** (over or more)	**trans-** (across)
antiseptic	intermediate	subzero	supermarket	transatlantic

♣ Choose a word that particularly appeals to you and weave a story round it. You might choose a title like 'Murder on the Transsiberian Express' or 'Submarine in distress'.

Name _____

Before and after

❖ Find out what **ante** and **post** mean. We use them a lot as prefixes in English and they alter the meaning of words completely.

❖ Write in whichever of the two you think belongs at the front of these words:

_ _ _ _ _ **cedent** means _____

_ _ _ _ _ **chamber** means _____

_ _ _ _ _ **date** means _____

_ _ _ _ _ **diluvian** means _____

_ _ _ _ _ **erity** means _____

_ _ _ _ _ **graduate** means _____

_ _ _ _ _ **humous** means _____

_ _ _ _ _ **meridiem** means _____

_ _ _ _ _ **natal** means _____

_ _ _ _ _ **pone** means _____

_ _ _ _ _ **script** means _____

_ _ _ _ _ **war** means _____

❖ Would both prefixes fit any of these words?

❖ **Pre** is another **pre**fix that comes in useful, for example **pre**heat. Hunt for more **pre** words and find out what they mean.

More or less

♣ Bearing in mind that **semi** means half and **multi** means many, find a word to fit each definition below.

A building with many storeys:

_____

Two houses joined together:

_____

A large crowd:

_____

Half a circle:

_____

A very, very rich person:

_____

When you are not fully awake:

_____

Speaking many languages:

_____

The last match before the championship:

_____

Something of many colours:

_____

A musical note:

_____

Something which has lots of different uses:

_____

Something that won't last forever:

_____

From many countries:

_____

When it's twilight:

_____

To increase in number:

_____

Gems like amethysts and garnets:

_____

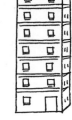

♣ Write what you would do if you were a **multi**millionaire. Try to include some of the words from your collection.

Name _____

Two's company

✤ Collect words beginning with the Latin prefixes **auto** meaning self and **co** meaning together, and write them in the laural wreaths.

✤ Discuss with your friend what each word means.

auto

autocrat
automobile

co

collide
combination

✤ Mark all the most important events on your lifeline.

I was born in 19......   Now   In the future?

✤ Write the first chapter of your autobiography on the back of this sheet.

Name _____

Braving the elements

Aqua and **hydro** mean water in Latin and Ancient Greek. **Aero** means air and **terra** means land.
❖ Work out with a friend what the words below might mean.

aquatic: _____

aquarium: _____

aqualung: _____

aqueduct: _____

dehydrated: _____

hydroelectricity: _____

hydrophobia: _____

hydrotherapy: _____

aerial: _____

aerodrome: _____

aerobics: _____

aerosol: _____

terracotta: _____

terrain: _____

extraterrestrial: _____

territory: _____

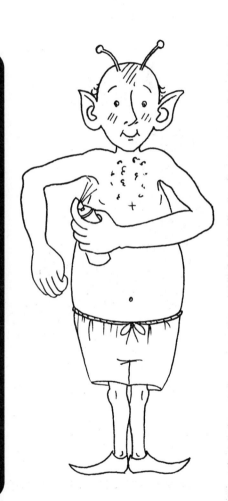

❖ Jumble up the letters and work out some clues to make a quiz. Try it out on your friends!

Borrowings

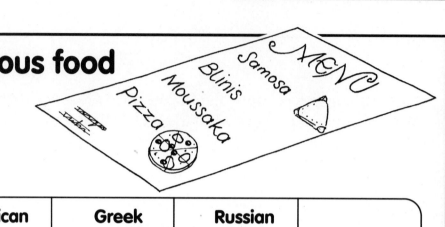

Food glorious food

❧ Look at the dishes on the menu. Which languages
have we borrowed these words from?

❧ Put them in the appropriate column below and
add as many other food words as you can.

French	Italian	Indian	Mexican	Greek	Russian	

Name _____

Daily bread

❖ Fill the shelves in the baker's shop with drawings of these products which come from all over the world.

nans   scones

buns   rolls

bagels   chapatti

blinis   croissants

cottage loaf   ciabatta

pitta   pikelet

matzo   sourdough

butties   tortilla

pizza   soda farl

granary   oatcake

pumpernickel   stottycake

baps   poppadom

baguette   girdlescone

puri

❖ Add items from your local baker's.
❖ Check the origins of the words you don't know.

❖ Start collecting bread recipes in a class book.

Name _____

It's a small world

♣ Below are some everyday words that have come to us from abroad.
Add as many other words as you can to the list.

From France	From Italy	From Spain
avalanche	confetti	palomino
ballet	espresso	patio
bureau	inferno	poncho
café	opera	siesta
chauffeur	piano	sombrero
garage	solo	
	stiletto	

♣ Make up your own quiz.
• Choose your favourite words from the lists.
• Write a definition for each one.
• Ask your friends to guess the word from the definition and say which of the three countries the word comes from. (You can give a first letter clue if you like.)

Teacher Timesavers: Spelling and language skills

Words from India

Many words came into the English language from Indian languages during the nineteenth century when India was part of the British colonial empire.
❖ Solve the clues to find out what some of these words are.

A game played on horseback:

p _ _ _

Spicy relish:

c _ _ _ _ _ _ _

Light brown:

k _ _ _ _

Overalls:

d _ _ _ _ _ _ _ _

For washing the hair:

s _ _ _ _ _ _

Riding breeches:

j _ _ _ _ _ _ _

Loose clothes for sleeping:

p _ _ _ _ _ _ _

Tropical forest:

j _ _ _ _ _

Single storey house

b _ _ _ _ _ _ _

Horseriding event:

g _ _ _ _ _ _ _

Hot dish:

c _ _ _ _

Bracelet:

b _ _ _ _ _

A boat with two hulls:

c _ _ _ _ _ _ _

Exercise for mind and body

y _ _ _

Small sailing boat:

d _ _ _ _ _ _

❖ Add any more words to the list that you can find.

Words from the USA

✤ Look at this collection of words. They come to us from Native North Americans, cowboys and modern USA.
✤ Decide where the words come from and write them down below.

Native American	Cowboys	Modern USA

bonanza
canoe
colt
corral
drive-in
hamburger
hijack
hot dog
moccasin
mustang
penthouse
potato
stetson
skyscraper
tomato
totem

✤ Hunt around for other words and add them to your lists.
✤ Write an adventure set in the days of the cowboys or in present-day America.

Name _____

Words from around the world

❖ Fill in the origins of these words as quickly as you can.
A dictionary will come in handy to check out your ideas or if you get stuck.

algebra –	nadir –
boss –	outlaw –
chalet –	panda –
devil – *Greek*	quadruped –
éclair –	rumour –
forum –	sauna –
geyser –	tom-tom –
hobble –	ugly – *Vikings*
interval –	voodoo –
ju-jitsu –	walkabout –
kiosk –	Xavier –
leprechaun –	yoga –
museum –	zero –

❖ Discuss with a friend what all the words mean.

❖ On the back of this sheet create your own alphabet quiz and try it out on your friends. Keep a dictionary handy for checking!

Name _____

My nan's cat

This is a game to play on wet wintry days when you can't go out to play.

♣ Go through the alphabet describing Nan's cat!

My nan's cat is an **angry** cat and her name is Arabella.

My nan's cat is a **beautiful** cat and her name is Belladonna.

My nan's cat is a **c**

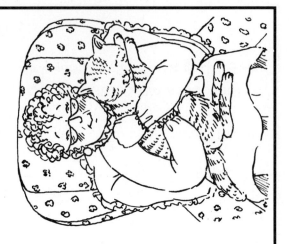

Name _____

Fun with -ful

Lots of adjectives end in **-ful** like aw**ful**, beauti**ful** and cheer**ful**.

❖ Collect as many of these words as you can in this doggy bag ready to play the game 'Next door's dog'.

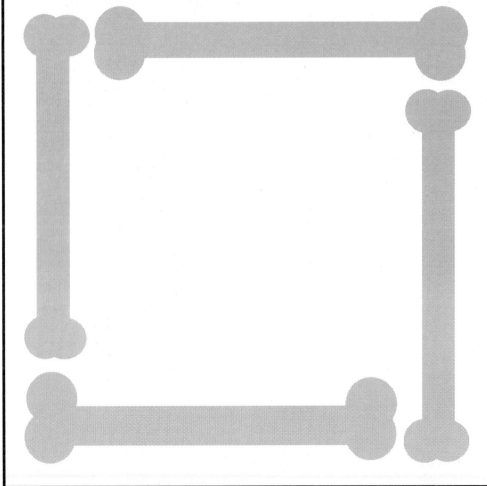

❖ Now, wander through the alphabet describing next door's dog – but only **-ful** words are allowed!

Next door's dog is an **awful** dog, a **bountiful** dog, a **careful** dog, a d_____ dog, an e_____ dog,

_____

_____

_____

_____

_____

_____

_____

_____

_____

_____

_____

Busy bees

Name _____

Busy bees

Be a busy bee and fly right through the alphabet!

❧ Choose a theme to write about, such as 'Going on a trip', or 'My class'.
Here's a starter for you...

Armajit **a**sked to go to the sea.

Bobby **b**egged to go too.

Carlton **c**hanged his mind three times.

Donna **d**ecided...

E

F

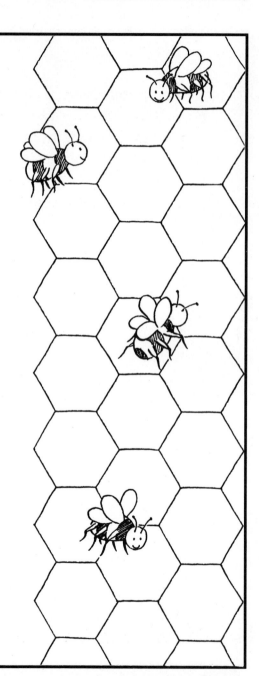

❧ Illustrate your sentences and make a book for your friends to read.

Name _____

Treasure trove

♣ Think of all the precious things your grandmother might have collected over the years. Hidden away in the attic is her trunk with all those treasures inside....

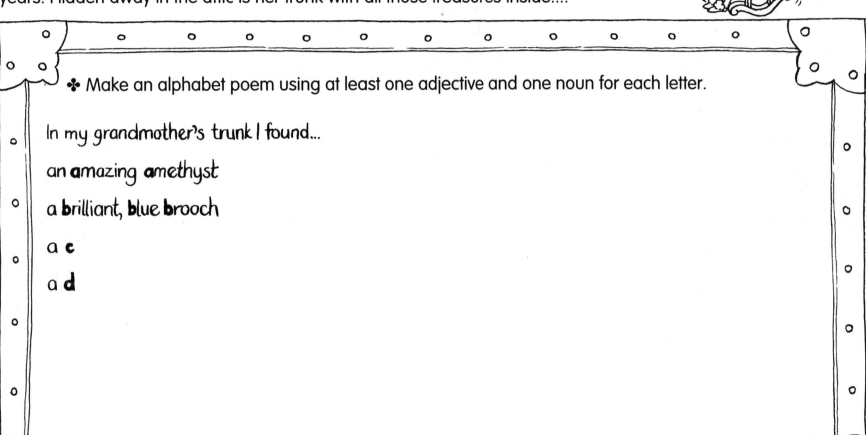

♣ Make an alphabet poem using at least one adjective and one noun for each letter.

In my grandmother's trunk I found...

an **amazing amethyst**

a **brilliant, blue brooch**

a **c**

a **d**

♣ Illustrate each treasure, design a cover and publish a new book to add to your class collection.

Alphabet calypso

Alphabet calypso

All around the world, early in the morning, people set off to market to buy bargains.
✤ Brainstorm foods that begin with all the letters of the alphabet.
✤ Clap out a calypso rhythm.
✤ Write your alphabet food song. You can continue the one below if you like.

Early in the morning, I went to the market; I went to market and I did buy

apples, appetising apples

bananas, beautiful bananas

c

✤ When you are satisfied with your song, add instruments and record it for an assembly.

Name _____

Spell it to music

♣ Make up as many words as you can from the musical notes A to G. You can use each letter more than once. It might help if you organise them alphabetically.

A	B	C	D
ace	bad bag		

E	F	G

G F E D C B A

♣ Now your friends can play your words on chime bars.
• Write the words clearly on a large sheet of paper.
• Conduct your orchestra through the list of words, pointing at each letter.
• Sing the letters together as the musicians strike the right chime bar.
• Keep a steady beat at first. You can speed up to make it more difficult, if you like.

Name _____

Pass the paper

Pass the paper

1st round	2nd round	3rd round
new water		

✤ Sit in a circle with a few friends and write down any word you like on the **1st round** strip such as 'new'.

✤ Pass the strip to the friend on your right who should write down a word that starts with the **last** letter of your word, such as **w**ater.

✤ Continue until you get your own strip back.

✤ Check the spellings together and put them right if necessary.

✤ Read your lists in turn and use the words to make up a story.

Change the rules and make it the last two letters next time.

Name _____

Crossword puzzles

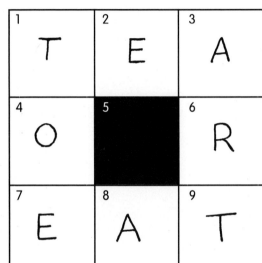

✤ Make up the clues for this crossword.

Across   **Down**

1   **1**

7   **3**

✤ Make up a crossword puzzle with a friend. Shade in the squares you don't need. Don't forget it's your job to make up the clues.

Across   **Down**

✤ Try again using more squares this time.

Name _____

Water puzzles

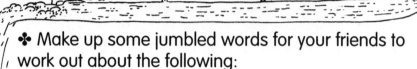

Water puzzles

♣ Unscramble the letters and work out these watery words.

elka ➝ _____   niar ➝ _____

dpno ➝ _____   verri ➝ _____

dolfo ➝ _____   encao ➝ _____

ase ➝ _____   woshre ➝ _____

pluded ➝ _____   loop ➝ _____

master ➝ _____

♣ Make up some jumbled words for your friends to work out about the following:
• what lives in the sea;
• what you find on the shore;
• what you can do with water.

➝

➝

➝

➝

➝

➝

➝

➝

➝

Name _____

Shannon's game

✤ Think of a word, then write the first letter and put dashes for the rest.

c _ _ _ _

✤ Ask your partner to guess the next letter.

• Give them two points if it's right;

ch ✓ = + 2

• Give them one point if it **could** be the start of an English word;

cr   = + 1

• Give them no points if it isn't an English letter string;

cp = 0

• Wild guesses lose a point!

cuckoo = -1

• A correct guess before all the letters are in place wins a bonus point.

child = + 1

• Carry on until the word is complete.

✤ Take it in turns to think of a word. Have fun!

PLAY HERE ↓

Name _____

Ghosts

A game of ghosts

♣ Play the game **ghosts** with a group of friends.

Rules
• Each player has five lives – one for every letter of GHOST.
• You lose a life when you complete a word.
• As you lose your lives you cross off the letters. When there are none left you are out of the game.

How to play
• The first player should write down a letter, for example **b**.
• The second player has to think quickly of a word starting with **b**, then writes the second letter, for example **a**.
• The third player must think of another word beginning with **ba**, then add the next letter, for example **b**.
• The fourth player has to think of a word starting with **bab**. If she thinks of the word **baby** and adds a **y**, then she has completed the word and loses a life. If she thinks of the word **babble** and adds **b**, then she is safe!
• Once a word is completed, the next player can start off with a new letter.

Think hard and stay alive as long as you can!

Here are your five lives: **G H O S T**

Now play here ➡

Name _____

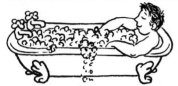

Collectors' paradise

♣ You have 15 minutes to write down all the words you can ga**the**r that have the letter pattern **the** in **the**m.

Some helpful hints:　• use the 'change a letter' technique, adding letters in front and behind;
　　　　　　　　　• add on prefixes and suffixes;
　　　　　　　　　• think of nouns, verbs, adjectives and adverbs.

bathe			
		lather	
			they
	fatherly		

♣ Try again using the pattern **act**, for example **act**or, c**act**us, re**act**ion and so on.
♣ Think of more little words or letter patterns you can use to play another time.

Palindromes

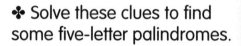

Palindromes

Palindromes are words that read the same backwards and forwards. Quite a lot of three-letter words are palindromes, for example, bib, Mum, Dad, Nan.

✤ Hunt for some more and write them here.

✤ Now try four-letter words. Try words which have **oo** or **ee** in the middle.

✤ Solve these clues to find some five-letter palindromes.

• **Clue:** it helps ships in the fog.

r _ _ _ _

• **Clue:** not hilly or bumpy.

l _ _ _ _

• **Clue:** for the people of the town.

c _ _ _ _

✤ Keep your **eye**s open for more!

Rhyming words

Have you noticed how much young children enjoy books that rhyme?
♣ Write a short rhyming story for the children in the reception class or local nursery.

♣ Let's start with **cat**. List as many words as you can that rhyme with cat.

bat
brat
chat

♣ Use your words to complete this story

The cat sat quietly on the mat until...

it saw _____

and _____

and _____

and _____

'Drat! Scat! Splat!' hissed the cat.

And that was the end of the

_____

Yes, that was the end of that.

♣ Make your story into a book. Illustrate each sentence and arrange the words and pictures carefully.

♣ Why not write some other rhyming books? You can start with any word – just get your rhyming list ready and off you go.

Name _____

Poets' corner

Poets' corner

✤ Find out where the families of all your classmates came from originally.

✤ Find words that rhyme with the place names, for example Jamaica: baker, maker, shaker.

Name	Family home	Rhyming words

✤ Make up a two-line poem – this is called a rhyming couplet – to describe your classmates like this one:

'She came from Jamaica
And her Daddy was a baker'.

✤ Now write your couplets over the page.

✤ Design a flag to go with the place names.

✤ Make a display with your collection of flags and rhyming couplets.

Rabbit and pork means rhyming talk

Cockneys invented rhyming slang so that no one else would understand what they were saying. They use a word that **rhymes** with the word they mean.

♣ Guess what these rhyming words mean.

apples and pears – *stairs*

north and south –

plates of meat –

trouble and strife –

lump of lead –

butcher's hook –

mutton pies –

frog and toad –

bread and cheese –

Cain and Abel –

♣ Invent some rhyming slang of your own. What would you say for:

dress –

shirt –

coat –

hat –

♣ Write a short story using rhyming slang instead of ordinary words and see if your friends can understand it.

Name _____

Quick thinking

Quick thinking

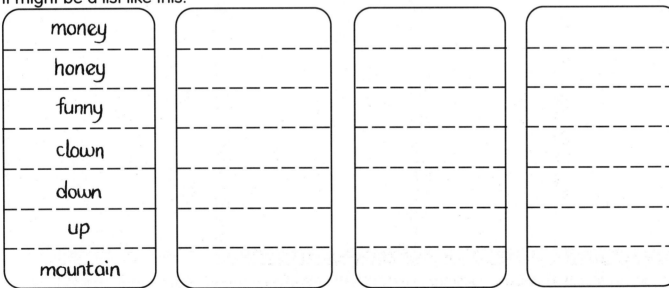

To make this game fun, you have to think as quick as a flash. You can use a stopwatch or give a count of three if you like. You'll get faster the more you play.

♣ Sit with some friends in a circle.

♣ Write down any word then pass the paper on to the friend on your right.

♣ That person writes a word that must **either** rhyme with the one on the paper **or** is connected with the meaning **or** means the opposite.

♣ When the paper comes back to you read out what is written. It might be a list like this:

money			
honey			
funny			
clown			
down			
up			
mountain			

♣ Turn over for more tries.

Onomatopoeia

Onomatopoeic words sound like what they mean like plop.

✤ Fill the notepads with onomatopoeic words which are used
to describe people and sounds around us.

Words describing people talking

Sounds all around us

✤ Use these words to write about a noisy day out – perhaps at a fair, or a swimming pool, or a trip to the seaside.

Spoonerisms

Spoonerisms

Reverend Spooner was famous because he used to mix up the letters in his words, which made them sound very funny.

♣ Say these spoonerisms to your friends and see if they can guess the nursery rhymes.

• Lary had a mittle lamb;

• Old King Cole was a serry old moul;

• Passy cut, passy cut, where have bou yeen?

• Sprack Jat could eat no fat.

♣ Make up some more spoonerisms to try out on your friends. For instance, how would you change:

• Girls and boys come out to play;

• The Grand Old Duke of York;

• Little Miss Muffet sat on a tuffet;

• Little Jack Horner sat in a corner.

♣ Keep going until you run out of nursery rhymes.

Name _____

Alliteration

Alliteration is when you use several words that start with the same **sound.**

♣ Finish the number poem below with lots of alliterations.

One	worried worm wiggled in the whirling water,
Two	troubled tortoises took the train to town,
Three	
Four	
Five	
Six	
Seven	
Eight	
Nine	
Ten	

♣ Tape record your poem so that everyone can enjoy listening to these sounds.

♣ If you have some ideas left over, write another alliterative poem.

Name _____

Homophones

Homophones

Homophones are words that **sound** the **same** but are spelled differently and have a different meaning.

✤ Link the pairs of homophones with a line.

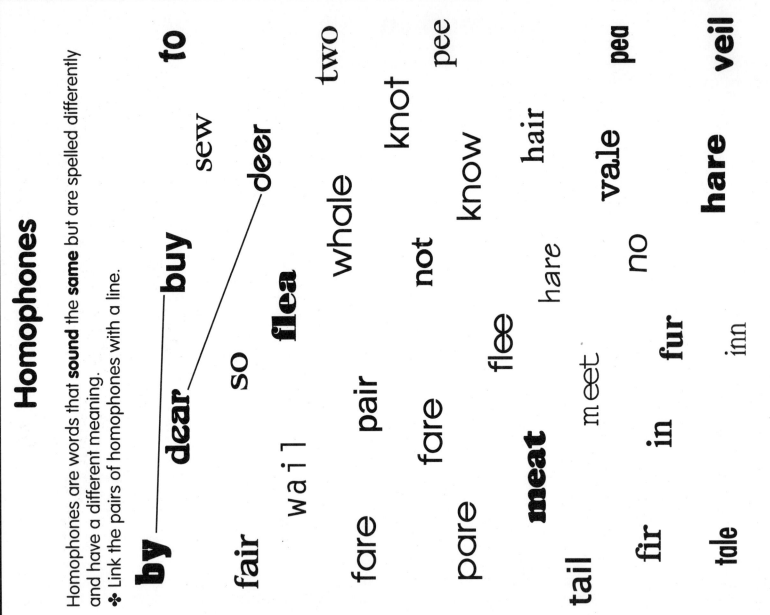

by   to

dear   buy   sew

fair   so   deer

flea

fare   pair   whale   two

knot

pare   fare   not   know   pee

flee   hare   hair

tail   meet   meat   vale   pea

fir   in   no

tale   fur   hare   hare   pea

inn   veil

✤ Take it in turns to describe one of the pairs and give a clue to the first letter. For example, "I'm thinking of a pair of homophones beginning with 'd', one is an animal and one you use when writing a letter'. [**Answer**: deer and dear].

• Score one point for guessing correctly.
• Score two more points for spelling **both** words correctly.

Name _____

Fun with puns

♣ Can you see the joke in these made-up book titles?
They all depend on **puns** – words that sound the same but
mean different things. Fill in the other meanings.

'Road Hog' by Laurie Dryver... (lorry driver)

'The Steep Cliff' by Eileen Dover... (_ _ _ _ _ _ _ _)

'The Haunted House' by Hugo First... (_ _ _ _ _ _ _)

'Pray for me' by Neil Downe... (_ _ _ _ _ _ _ _)

'Keep Fit' by Jim Nastics... (_ _ _ _ _ _ _ _)

'Keep it up' by Lucy Lastic... (_ _ _ _ _ _ _ _ _)

'Victorian Transport' by Orson Kart... (_ _ _ _ _ _ _)

'Open House' by Colin Ennityme... (_ _ _ _ _ _ _)

'The Treasure Chest' by Anne Teaks... (_ _ _ _ _ _ _)

'Frank Conquers the World' by Betty Duzzant... (_ _ _ _ _ _)

♣ Make a book of jokes with your friends based on puns.

Name _____

Lost consonants

Lost consonants

♣ Spot which consonant has been missed out to make the joke.

• Every year they spent their two weeks holiday in pain.   [S ←Spain]

• He loved his grandma very much and always tried to lease her.   [_ ← _ _ _ _ _ _]

• He had a grand time playing with his toy cane.   [_ ← _ _ _ _ _]

• Puffing and panting, we arrived two minutes late for the rain.   [_ ← _ _ _ _ _]

♣ Make up some more funny sentences like this and test them out on your friends.

•

•

•

•

♣ You can do illustrations to go with them to make them even funnier!

Synonyms

Synonyms are words that mean the same. A thesaurus is a very useful book to help you find synonyms.

♣ Fill the gaps with words associated with sad feelings.

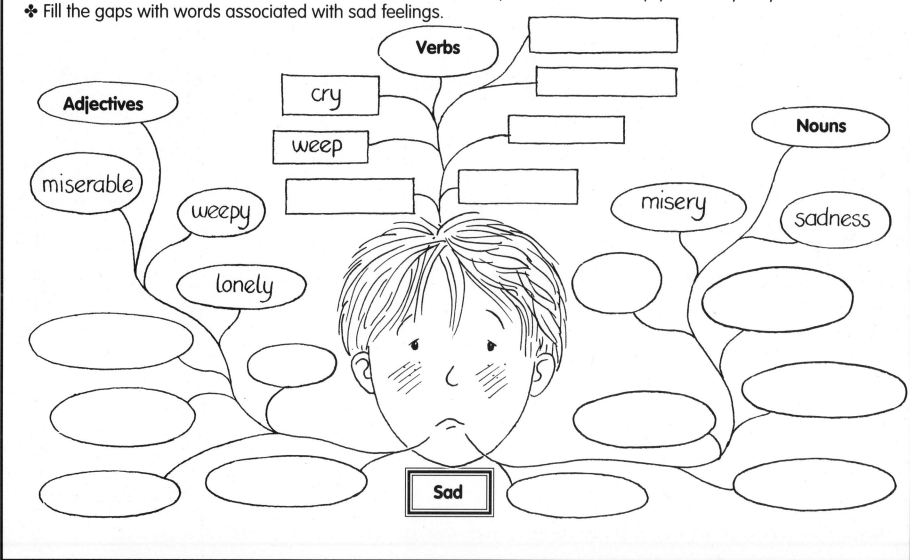

Name _____

Went

Word power

Went is a very overused word. Think of all the different ways you can move: you can **bump**, **chase**, **dash** and so on.

♣ List below in alphabetical order all the ways you can move.

Arrive	**N**
B	**O**
C	**P**
Dart	**Q**
E	**R**
F	**S**tride
G	**T**
H	**U**
I	**V**
Jog	**W**
K	**X**
L	**Y**
M	**Z**

♣ **Said** is another well-worn word. List all the other words you can use instead like **shouted**, **whispered**....

Antonyms

Antonyms are words that mean the opposite of each other.
♣ Race through this alphabetical list and give the antonyms.
You can use a thesaurus to help you.

Awful:

Brave:

Childish:

Daring:

Everlasting:

Fat:

Grumpy:

Heavy:

Inside:

Junior:

Kind:

Lovely:

Merry:

Naughty:

Open:

Private:

Quick:

Restful:

Silent:

Terrible:

Usual:

Vexed:

Windy:

eXcited:

Young:

Zany:

EXCITED: BUSY, BUSTLING, RUSHING, ACTIVATED

♣ Now challenge your friends. Do one list for adjectives or adverbs, one list for nouns and one list for verbs.

Homographs

Homographs

Homographs are words that are spelled the same but sound different and have a different meaning, like tear and tear.

❧ Solve these riddles to find the homographs.

I begin with **R**.
One of me is a neat line.
The other is a noisy argument.

_____

I begin with **B**.
One of me is worn in the hair.
The other is a way of greeting
important people.

_____

I begin with **S**.
One of me is a female pig.
The other is a job for a farmer.

_____

I begin with **L**.
One of me is metal.
The other one shows the way.

_____

I begin with **R**.
One of me is a town in Berkshire.
The other is having fun with a book.

_____

tear

tear

❧ Now it's your turn to
make up some riddles.

Name _____

Similes

Similes

Similes are a good way of describing things by comparing them with something else, by saying they are **like** or **as** something else. We use them all the time.

❧ Finish off these **similes** as fast as you can.

as black as_____

as white as_____

as quick as_____

as blind as a_____

as strong as a_____

as weak as a_____

as clean as a_____

as cool as a_____

as bright as a_____

❧ When we use the same similes over and over again, they lose their power and become **clichés**. Now try the list again but think more carefully and make some more unusual comparisons.

as black as

as white as

as quick as

as blind as a

as strong as a

as weak as a

as clean as a

as cool as a

as bright as a

❧ Write a description of a friend using similes.

Name _____

Similes galore!

Similes galore!

We often describe people's behaviour by comparing them to other things, especially animals.

✤ Discuss with a friend, then write down what these similes really mean:

• like a bear with a sore head →

• like a bull in a china shop →

• like a cat on hot bricks →

• like a cow on a bike →

• like a ship in full sail →

• like a child with a new toy →

✤ Now make up your own similes that mean the same thing:

✤ Draw pictures to illustrate your similes.

Figures of speech

Sometimes we use phrases that don't quite say what they mean!
❖ Look at these pictures and you'll get the idea.

a storm in a teacup

a bee in her bonnet

hopping mad

❖ Now it's your turn. Draw a picture to illustrate the sayings below:

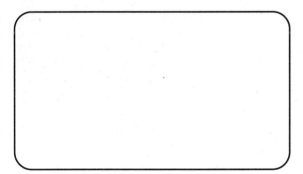

blowing his own trumpet

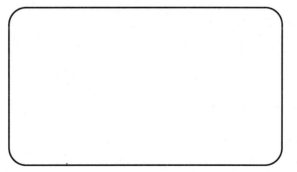

like a dog with two tails

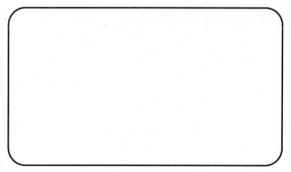

a flea in your ear

❖ Discuss with your friend what these sayings really mean.
❖ Think of some more and illustrate them on a large sheet of paper.
❖ Mount a display of everyone's illustrations.

Old favourites

Old favourites

It's interesting to collect well-known sayings.

✣ Have some fun with sayings about time.

Here are some to get you going:

'Time waits for no man'

'Time flies'

'Time stood still'

✣ Now make a collection for your own class topic.

✣ There are lots more topics you could try: weather/places/colours/clothes/play.